I Decree and Declare For the Apostolic *And* Kingdom Minded

I Decree and Declare For the Apostolic *And* Kingdom Minded

Elder Michelle Fordyce-Jackson

Copyright © 2012 by Elder Michelle Fordyce-Jackson.

Library of Congress Control Number: 2012912659
ISBN: Hardcover   978-1-4771-4307-0
       Softcover   978-1-4771-4306-3
       Ebook   978-1-4771-4308-7

All rights reserved. No part of this book may be reproduced or transmitted in any form or by any means, electronic or mechanical, including photocopying, recording, or by any information storage and retrieval system, without permission in writing from the copyright owner.

This book was printed in the United States of America.

To order additional copies of this book, contact:
Xlibris Corporation
1-888-795-4274
www.Xlibris.com
Orders@Xlibris.com

Contents

Acknowledgement 11
Spirit of Prayer 13
Demonic and Generational Curses 14
Spirit of Nabal Foolishness 17
Spirit of Judas 17
Spirit of Rejection 18
Spirit of Religion 18
Seducing Spirit 19
Spirit of Sexual Perversion 20
Homosexuality & Lesbian Spirit 20
Masturbation 21
Spirit of Pornography 21
Spirit of Suspicion 22
Spirit of Jealousy 23
Spirit of Deception 24
Unclean Spirits 24
Call of Release 25
Daily Declaration of God Reveal To me 26
Daily Declaration of Expectations 27
Declaration for True Worship & Praise 27
Transformation 28
Exercising Our Authority 30
Biblical Dominion 30
Push Me To Purpose 32
Thankful 33
Peace In My Spirit 34
Fleshly Desires 34
Sinners Prayer 35
The Hand Of God 35
Unsaved Loved Ones 36
Prayer for Forgiveness 36

Prayer to set free	36
Prayer Against Suicide	37
Daily Temptations	37
Return to What	38
I Decree That Death Is the Gift Of A Finisher	40
Daily Declaration	41
A Prophetic Release of the Four Winds	42
God in Me	43
Prophetic Me	44
My Children	46
Spirit of Sheba	48
Being Obedient to the Heavenly Vision	49
I'm Free	50
I'm Not Looking Back	51
I Speak To My Mind	53
Second Wind of My Destiny	53
God Given Direction	55
Clarion Call of God's People	57
I Decree My Billions	58
Divine Invitation for a Divine Season	59
I'm Not Going To Hell	60
The Rain of God	61
My Heavenly Deposit	63
I'm a Child of Destiny and Purpose	63
He Kept Me	65
The Voice	66
My Powerful Covenant	67
My Apostolic Impartation	69
My Apostolic Culture	71
Refresh Me	71
The Fire of God	72
I Will Immerse In the Glory	74
Spiritual Waters over Me	75
Canceling the Attacks from Hell	76
Wait on the Timing of God	78
Apostolically Walking Stable	79
Apostle Heart	80
My Spiritual Mate	82
Apostolic Momentum	83
Recognize, Raise, Reform and Release	84
What Happens When I don't Study	86
Exercising Your Authority	86

Demonic Flies	87
Demonic Crabs	88
Demonic Eyeballs	89
Power of Being Unified	89
Momentum	91
My Past Does Not Matter	92
Ruling in The Midst of My Enemy's	93
Govern to Grace	94
Transformational Thinker	94
Who Am I	95
The Blood Over My Incarcerated Child	96
I'm God on Earth	98
Prophetic Atmosphere	98
I Must Qualify the People Around Me	100
Gateway Churches	102
I'm Walking in A Season Of No Drawbacks	104
Manifesting Prophetic Purpose	105
Deep Sea Fishing	106
Amalekites Spirits	107
Gods Prophecy	108
Dung Gate	108
What God Says for This Season	109
Anointed to Destroy and Pull Down	110
Fruit of an Apostolic House	110
My Election For Repentance	112
The Cross I Bare	113
My Haters	114
Keeper Of the Flame	115
Gods Glory Shall Return	116
Spirit of Elijah	117
Soulish Prophecy	117
My Prayer Life	119
Elected for Promotion	120
Religion Has No Place in Apostolic	121
I Must Die To My Flesh	122
All Burdens Not Bad	123
What God is Saying	124
What God Wants In This Season	125
The Next Move Of God	126
Promises For My Offspring	127
God's Covenant	128
I Have a Right To Be Free From My Past	129

Dark Places of Rebellion 130
My Covenant Will Allow Me To.. 131
Walking Blindly 132
A Breakthrough Believer 132
Move In A Strong Apostolic Relationship 134
Obedience in All... 135
Breaking The Spirit of Limitations 136
Mobilizing My Child For the Apostolic 137
What God Excepts From Me 139
Atmosphere For Encouraging Myself 140
Testing The Word Over Your Life 141
Can God Use My Womb 142
What Makes You Apostolic 143
The Announcement Has Been Made 144
Walking Through My Open Door.. 145

In Loving Memory of
Robert & Dorothy Butler (grandparents)
Wm Billy Smith Jr (brother)
Thalia Lynn Barber (cousin)
Ellis & Millie Bruce (grandparents)
Rochelle (Shelly) Thomas (cousin)
Marshall Bruce (uncle)

Acknowledgement

It is our desire that in the pages of this book you will catch a personal glimpse of the power of prayer from an apostolic and prophetic perspective. In this book you will find power the power of prayer.

This book is not about proving theological points; it is a book that will show you how to have the kind of prayer life that gets results. This book is more of a manual of instruction and inspiration for those hungry to see more of the reality and power of God's flow in their lives, which comes from prayer.

Here you will find Elder Michelle Jackson releases to you strong prayers, which come from pain, struggles, and triumphs. You may be a person who wants to help meet needs in your own life or in those of your family and friends, well this is the book that will help you.

As you read on, it is our prayer that the King of Glory will give you instruction, inspiration, and a fresh anointing in prayer, to do great exploits for the kingdom of God.

Apostle Melvin & Tashya Thompson

I dedicate this book to all the apostolic kingdom believers that speak and walk with their God given authority. To my sons Jay & Jordan Wilkerson Jordan there is a word in you that is ready for your generation. When God gets done with you it will all make sense the nation is waiting for you son.
Special thanks to these mighty women who never stop praying for me when I couldn't pray for myself: Mary Washington, Yvonne Bruce, Mattie Smith, Cynthia Butler, and Drusilla (Auntie Pat) Watts.

On February 18, 2012 I married my gift from heaven William J Jackson you are the one from God my soul mate forever. We have the nations to go to. Thank you being patient with me, believing in me, and buying me the new laptop that I wrote this book on. When I don't understand myself you understand me. Like Apostle Thompson said "God has given you the grace to deal with me".

I want to thank God for all he has built on the inside of me. For looking beyond my faults and seeing the greatness he predestined me for. When God gave me the unction to write a book of decrees it all came together in less than three months. God would speak to me everywhere in the movies, bathroom, expressway . . . etc. I would write down God's thoughts on receipts, toilet paper, my hand, it was an amazing journey. God knew that I understood what it meant to decree and declare a thing over my life. For years I spoke what I wanted to take place into my life and my family and friends lives. In 2006 I was introduced to the television ministry of Apostle John Eckhart and learned so much about demonic & spiritual warfare a calling that God had placed on my life and I didn't understand it. In 1999 God told me I'm going to send you into the nations and regions to break through strong holds and principalities that control cities, regions, and denominations. God told me you are going to pray and decree and declare and the kingdom of darkness will be broken.

It has not been a bed of roses the devil is still the devil. I went through back breaking trials & tribulations, the death of my brother, family coming against me, my children took me through. My parents never accepted me from my childhood into my adulthood. My change was always acting strange. I was lied on, and my previous church only wanted me for the talent God gave me. Through it all I survived and character was built in me. I learned to love and forgive myself.

God used it all so I could open my mouth and declare his word. So when I minister I can teach from the vein of been there done that.

I would love to thank my spiritual father and mother in the gospel Apostle Melvin & Apostle Tashya Thompson of All Nations Evangelist Church in Harrisburg, PA. Through the support and unconditional love that was showed to me I was able to be the women that God called me to be. No one understands the "DIVA" like my All Nations Family. My love to Henrietta, Dee, both Keisha's, Erica, Sharrod, Amy, Glen, June, Valerie, Bro Dee, Chanda, Shawn, Tonyce, Thomanisa, Velma & sister, Alana, Brykeisha, Neicey, Chardae, Fummi, Ola, Gloria, Pastor Jackie Bethea, Sara, Markie, Prophetess Wolfe, Jeanne, Nedra, Michelle, Sonya, Kim, Yolanda, Daishya, A.J. and Shakera. Just to name a few I love you from the bottom of my heart.

To Michael, Marvin, and Mark Washington a girl could not ask for a special set of brothers who always looks out for Big Sis. To my favorite uncle Meal a.k.a Scrooge love you.

Author photo courtesy of: Sara Vogelson

Spirit of Prayer

Through my prayers I welcome Jesus into my life I'm giving God permission to interfere with earth's affairs in prayer.
I recognize that Jesus is the authoritative one in my life; my spirit man will receive from Jesus in prayer.
I will ask God about everything in prayer and supplication.
I will pray and not lose heart.
I will hear God clearly before making any decisions in every area of my life.
My prayers are meant to be answered; I will remind God of his promises he spoke over my life.
God I will pray your word over my life; I believe your word will not come back to you void. My life has purpose and a meaning.
I declare that I will pray anytime and anywhere.
I will not doubt and fear what I ask for in prayer.
Waiting for my prayers to be answered stretches my faith in God.
I declare that whatever I ask in the name of Jesus he's going to do it.
I declare that I will not limit how God responds.
I decree and declare that I can tap into the power of God through prayer.
I declare that I have authority and dominion in prayer.
I declare that I will reach a point of prayer that the devil can't locate me.
True prayer will usher me into the presence of God.
I will embrace the power of God through prayer.
I decree that the word of God will become real in my spirit man.
I decree and declare no demonic force can stop me from getting into the presence of God
I nullify all spirits of depression, guilt; not tithing that can block my prayers from being answered.
John 15:7 If ye abide in me, andp my words abide in you, ye shall ask what ye will, and it shall be done unto you.

Demonic and Generational Curses

I declare that every judgment that came to me through generational curse is broken.
No generational curse will reduce my quality of life or take it away.
I have addressed all sins in my life; Father God if there is any hidden sin in bloodline let it be exposed now in the name of Jesus.
God has forgiven all past iniquity and transgression in my life.
No failure, shame, sickness and even physical death shall come to me in the name of Jesus.
I will repent and find restoration and a renewed freedom from the Lord.
I will not rebel to any hidden sin that God has revealed to me.
I declare that all my personal sin will be revealed in the name of Jesus.
I decree that all my past sin is under the blood of Jesus.
I will not allow satan to cause grief in my life because of generational sins and curses.
All curses in my blood line are broken in the name of Jesus.
I declare that I will confess and acknowledge my sins when they are exposed by God.
I will not give satan any legal claim to my life through generational sin.
My legal authority is what makes me an overcomer of demonic curses.
The blood of the Lamb cancels my generational curses.
I'm an overcomer by the word of my testimony and my intercession.
Rev 12:11 And they overcame him by the blood of the Lamb, and by the word of their testimony; and they loved not their lives unto the death.
The threefold cord of spiritual bondage is broken off my life in the name of Jesus.
Every curse magnet that attracts the demonic realm is broken off of my life in the name of Jesus.
I will not open my spirit to the demonic realm through disobedience in the name of Jesus.
I declare that I'm set free and cleansed from all unrighteousness.
Every false curse that came through religion is broken off me in the name of Jesus.
The enemy cannot destroy my destiny or birthright in the name of Jesus.
I break the root of bitterness and anger in my blood line.
Through Jesus I am delivered.

I curse every familiar spirit and spirit guide that have connected to me through generational curses and have followed my life. I blind you and command that you are silenced and removed from my life.
The blood of Jesus will kill the curses on my life.
I declare that satan will not have his way in my life through curses.
I walk in complete forgiveness so any spoken curses will not be able to take root in my life.
I will stop judging other so I will not curse my own life.
I will not be cursed due to my ignorance.
The Spirit of God can intercede for cursed people.
I curse every agent of satan that spoke a cures over my life, family, spouse, children and siblings. I nullify these word and they are void and have no life or meaning.
I cancel every time released curse in my life. By the blood of Jesus I am not cursed.
I decree that every curse that comes from a written curse, curses spoken in secret, rebellion, false beliefs, oaths, vows, pacts with satan, curses on my finances, confusion, rejection, sexual sins are cancelled in the name of Jesus I'm set free.
I curse at the root every curse off my family that comes from playing cards which is a tool of satan.
I cancel all curses from abominable things in my house in the name of Jesus.
I have separated myself from all unbelievers and all unclean things. I will no longer bring curses upon myself.
I will not allow any statues of owls, frogs, unicorns, dragons, horseshoes, and Buddha statues in my home.
I will remove all demonic items passed down from my ancestors any good luck charms, Oriental objects, items used in witchcraft, fortune cookies, other religions (doctrines of devils) in my home in Jesus name.
I decree that I will not follow any demonic fads and will not let my children wear demonic symbols in their clothes.
I will not wear any jewelry associated with witchcraft, and demonic oppression.
I will not acknowledge any broken cross (peace sign), wishbones, stars, and clovers in the name of Jesus.
I renounce any involvement with Freemasons, Elks, or Legions from myself and ancestor involved in Jesus name.
I will not seek anything supernatural outside of Jesus.
The blood of Jesus has terminated this contract in my generation line.
I plead the Precious Blood against every curse and destroy at their roots and cast down each and every negative word, negative thoughts, fears, doubts,

I decree that any generational curse will not manifest in my life, and all demonic psychic attacks, psychic operations, or psychic assignments this day, any day past, or any day to come along with all acts of evil or witchcraft spoken against me, formed against me or directed against me in Jesus name. I decree that they shall never come to past, or interfere with my life and generations to come; every demonic demon is cursed at the root assigned to myself and family. t t

Spirit of Nabal Foolishness

I break the spirit of Nabal in the name of Jesus. I curse every spirit of foolishness in the name of Jesus.
I curse at the root every spirit of bitterness, anger, unforgiveness, cruelty, foolishness, and stupidity associated with the spirit of Nabal.
I decree from this day forward I walk in the spirit of forgiveness, love, and kindness.
I break every spirit of madness and confusion in the name of Jesus.
I'm forgiven for all my mistakes, and the way I have treated my fellow brothers and sisters in Christ.
I will not let a spirit of stupidity enter my spiritual realm.
I declare from this day forward I will walk in a spirit of cooperation, peace, patience, love, and humility.
I will always respond in a spirit of kindness.

Spirit of Judas

I break the spirit of Judas off the kingdom in the name of Jesus.
I declare that the spirit of Judas will not violate the apostolic move of the kingdom.
I silence this spirit from passing on information to my enemies about me in the name of Jesus.
I break off every symptoms of lust, love of money, unfaithfulness, betrayal, treason, deception, worldliness, and double mindedness associate with the spirit of Judas.
I bind the spirit of Judas and lose the spirit of order, unity, the mind of Christ, submission, protocol, faith, unity, and hope in Jesus name.
I cancel all rebellious spirits that come against God's divine and delegated authority.
I command this spirit to give honor and respect to all leaders in the body of Christ.
I declare that this spirit must openly challenge and defeated by the blood of Jesus.
As an apostolic church and region shaker we force the spirit of Korah out of the kingdom of God.

Spirit of Rejection

I break the spirit of rejection off my life in Jesus name. I will no longer be bound by the spirit of rejection.
I will deal with people who celebrate me and not tolerate me.
I declare that I will accept the truth that God made me beautiful on the inside and out.
I can give affection and receive affection.
I will no longer measure people by the worldly standards.
I declare that I can look in the mirror and say I love me.
I will not be bound by past rejection and hurts.
I declare I'm an overcomer of things designed to destroy me in Jesus name.
I refuse to go through life aimlessly with no direction.
I acknowledge my true worth and dignity. My worth does not depend on another individual.
I am worthy in God.
From this day forward I'm letting go of every negative person in my life.
I bind every spirit associated with the spirit of rejection denial, sadness, codependency, isolation, overweight, repression, disorder, sex for love, emptiness, lashing out, shame, hopelessness, and suicide in the name of Jesus.
I lose the spirit of love, peace, hope, deliverance, healing, and forgiveness in Jesus name.

Spirit of Religion

I declare that I am set free from a spirit of religion.
I break the spirit of religion in the body of Christ in Jesus name.
I break every spirit of Barabas off the body of Christ so they can no longer make scape goats in the kingdom of God.
I assonate every spirit of religion in the demonic realm in the name of Jesus the blood is against you.
I apply the blood of Jesus to the doorpost of my soul.
I will not allow a religious spirit to kill my momentum.
I break the assignment of every demonic fly attracted to my anointing in the name of Jesus.
I accept the label of victorious that God called me to.
I will not allow the spirit of religion to stop me from being a region shaker.
I declare I'm mission minded, free from critism, and I'm a risk taker.

I'm converted to be kingdom minded.
I declare I'm prophetic and apostolic minded.
I'm free from cursing and assonating people with my mouth.
I will not have a holier than thou attitude.
I will not be unteachable and break all rebellion off my life.
I will not operate in a spirit of control nor will I be controlled.
I renounce all doctrine of devils that I have allowed into my life.
I will not receive any false revelations.
I am healed from all spiritual adultery.
I'm set free from ritualism I will allow the Holy Spirit to have free reign in my church.
My church will not operate in traditionalism.
I release a spirit of truth, prophetic anointing an utterance, and the gift of discerning of spirits.

Seducing Spirit

I break the seducing spirit off of my life in the name of Jesus.
I close every demonic gate that has been open in my life to this seducing spirit.
I will not walk in a spirit of perversion, homosexuality, or lesbian.
I will not accept any counterfeit anointing over my life.
I break off every demonic confederacy associated with the spirit of seducing.
I sever my ties with any seducing spirit.
I will have no association with a seducing spirit.
I will not be lead down a path of destruction in the name of Jesus.
I declare I will not be seduced into submission.
I declare and decree every stronghold associated with the seducing spirit is broken in Jesus name.
I will not be enslaved to a life of sin.
I declare I will not fall under a demonic influence nor will I give in to its temptation.
Satan will not be able to temp me with his knowledge.
I declare that the seducing spirit will not manifest as enticement, escape, and allurement.
1 Timothy 4:1
Now the Spirit speaketh expressly, that in the latter times some shall depart from the faith, giving heed to seducing spirits, and doctrines of devils.
I release a spirit of truth, the anointing of the Holy Spirit, the wrath of God and a prophetic anointing in the name of Jesus.

Spirit of Sexual Perversion

I will not go against God's plan for sexual intimacy.
I decree and declare that no sexual perversion will be deposited in my spiritual man.
I will not be a host to sexual perversion.
I will not be aroused by the same sex.
I declare that sexual perversion will not be birthed in my generation.
I will stand in the gap and intercede for all rapist, homosexuals, and pedophiles, those that practice bestiality in the name of Jesus.
I ask God to expose are those in the pulpit and congregation that operate under this spirit.
I will not submit to the will of sexual perversion.
I will not be deceived or seduced by sexual perversion.
I decree that God will show me what proper love is in the name of Jesus.
I cancel the assignment of any demon trying to release sexual perversion on our youth.
I break the assignment of divorce and adultery in my bloodline due to sexual perversion.
I break the bastard curse off of my family in the name of Jesus.
Satan will not make me lower than an animal through sexual perversion. I will not have sex with no animals in the name of Jesus.
I declare that I will operate with the mind of Christ, every perverted desire and thought is cast down in the name of Jesus. Father God cleanse me with your blood.
I break every stronghold that will take me further away from the spirit of God.

Homosexuality & Lesbian Spirit

I break every homosexual and lesbian spirit off of my life in the name of Jesus. I will not allow this sprit to invade my life and take root.
I am delivered from the spirit of deception that would cause me to think the gay lifestyle is okay.
I renounce all same sex spirits and with the blood of Jesus I'm delivered and set free from any and all attractions to the same sex.
I accept the fact that I was not born gay.
I repent from any involvement with homosexual and lesbian lifestyle. God has forgiven me.

I will not fall prey to any unnatural desire in Jesus name.
I believe that every unholy desire is coming from demonic nature.
I declare that living in a gay lifestyle is an abomination to God.
I will use my sexual organs the way God intended for me to use them.
Only God has the power to set me free from a gay lifestyle. I will allow the Holy Spirit to work in my life.
God is not a respecter of persons.
I repent from being a woman walking around masculine like a man.
I repent from being a man trying to be feminine like a woman.
I repent for trying to trying to put an attack on the institution of family in Jesus name.
I break every ungodly soul tie through homosexuality by the blood of Jesus.
I close every door in my life that I left open for this spirit to enter in.
I break the curse of masturbation over my life that can open the door for homosexuality in Jesus name.,
I will not release semen as a sacrifice to satan through masturbation.

Masturbation

Father God I ask that I be delivered from the spirit of masturbation.
I will not have sex outside of marriage.
With the help of Jesus I will die to my selfish fleshly desires.
My eyes have been open to the sin of masturbation and I repent of my sins.
Sexual immorality is a sin against my own body.
I will never get to a place where I don't need God.
I will no longer stimulate myself with objects other than my hand.
I will not let the spirit of masturbation rob me of true worship.
I declare that I will be intimate with God until my mate arrives.
I will be sensitive to the touch of God.
Only God alone can give me the desires of my heart in Jesus name.

Spirit of Pornography

I declare that I will not allow the spirit of pornography to destroy me or my family.
I will not allow pornography destroy/pervert/ or twist the family institution that God has ordained on earth.

I curse every spirit associated with pornography lust, rape, incest, harlotry, adultery, and homosexuality in the name of Jesus.
I'm set free from the bondage of sexual sin I will not fall deeper into hardcore sexual sin.
I repent from ever being involved with pornography.
Father God I ask that you set free every child that is being used in child pornography.
God I ask that you have mercy on the adults that abuse children in a sexual way and bring deliverance into their life.
I will no longer lust at people in my mind; I have the mind of Christ.
I will not allow this spirit to undermine and distorts my moral and spiritual judgment.
Father God I cancel the war between spirit and flesh and I cover myself with the blood of Jesus.
I declare that I will not fall under the spirit of adultery in the name of Jesus.
Your word tells me to abstain from fornication.
I will no longer go against God's moral laws.
God I know that I am sanctified and set free.
I will not allow no demon to tell me that pornography is innocent fun.
No longer will I be a slave to any demonic forces in Jesus name.
I will not allow satan to whisper satanic thoughts into my mind.
I will not believe the lies from the pits of hell.
I will cast down any thoughts that are contrary to the word of God.
I decree and declare that I will no longer reason with sin.
My heart is fully submitted to God.
I have been drawn away from my own lusts.
Father God I ask that you fully deliver me from this sexual sin.
I am set me free from any and all evil spirits that have attached themselves to me because of my involvement in this activity.
Satan you are a liar, murder, and a deceiver in the name of Jesus I rebuke you satan with the blood of Jesus.
I renounce any involvement with pornography and sexual perversion in the name of Jesus.

Spirit of Suspicion

Father God in Jesus name I repent from allowing the spirit of suspicion to rule in my life.
I declare that I will not operate under the spirit of suspicion I will operate under the trust of God.

I repent for being suspicious of innocent people.
My eyes will not operate under suspicion my eyes will be spiritually open for the kingdom of God.
I will operate under the mind of Christ.
I will no longer be skeptical of everything and everybody. I cancel that assignment over my life now in the name of Jesus.
The wounds and breaks and tears in my heart have been healed through the blood of Jesus.
I will no longer isolate my mind from the truth.
I will not walk in a spirit of misunderstanding I will walk in the spirit of wisdom and the knowledge of God.
I bind the spirit of paranoia off my life I release a spirit of faith over my life.
I will not gossip and be judgmental of kingdom believers.
My hope and trust is in the Lord.
I will not allow my mind to operate under imagination.
I break every spirit of distrust, discord, alienation, anxiety, isolation, presumption, and prejudice off of my life in Jesus name.
I release the spirit of restoration, harmony, honesty and faith over my life in Jesus name.

Spirit of Jealousy

I renounce the spirit of Jealousy and pride off of my life in Jesus name.
I close any open door in my life to the spirit of lying in Jesus name.
I cancel this demonic stronghold off of my life right now in Jesus name.
I declare that the spirit of jealousy will no longer run rampant in the body of Christ.
I will walk with a heart of love and servant hood toward Jesus.
I will learn to love the very one I was jealous of.
The spirit of jealousy will no longer dominate church conversations.
My mind and heart will not close down but will be open to do the will of God.
I will literally love the hell out of someone that operates in a jealous spirit.
I command every spirit in common backbiting, belittling, bickering, bitterness, blasphemy, selfishness, spite, stealing, strife, suicide, suspicion, temper, unforgiveness, unworthiness, violence. cruelty, cursing, deception, destruction, discontent, disputes, dissatisfaction, distrust to go back to the pits of hell and to never return in Jesus name.

Spirit of Deception

I command every spirit of deception to break its grips off the kingdom of God.
Every stronghold of deception is broken my life in the name of Jesus.
No doorway or gaps will be let open for the spirit to return.
I will not allow my inner voice to speak deception into my life. I silence the voice of the accuser in the name of Jesus.
No fallen angels will deceive me I will not allow the world or the church to deceive me.
I know that satan was the biggest deceiver of them all I will not work for the kingdom of darkness.
In latter times I will not follow any deceiving spirits.
I decree that no deceiving spirit will work or play with my mind.
I decree that my own fleshly desires will not deceive me.
I will no longer allow my will to deceive me.
I must confront the spirit of deception in my family, church, marriage, friend and those in authority in control.
God please expose every evil person trying to deceive me that they will no longer be in my life.
No wounds from my past will lead me to deception.

Unclean Spirits

I decree and declare I will no longer be a gateway or door keeper for any unclean spirits reign over my life, my city, my region, my nation, and my church in the name of Jesus.
I will not be involved with any sexual innuendoes.
I will live a full life I declare this in Jesus name.
I will not die by my own lust in Jesus name.
I cancel every perverted nature of any unclean spirit.
No unclean spirit will stop me from serving God with all my heart.
I will not be involved in any lewd conversation and any filthy environment in Jesus name.
I declare that this spirit will not contaminate my anointing or undermine my anointing.
I will not let any demonic force twist or pervert nor cause any violence in my life.
No unclean spirit will determine my dress code I declare this in Jesus name.

I declare that no unclean spirit will violate our children and young adults.
I stop any unclean spirit from influencing my generation and generations to come in the name of Jesus.
Satan the blood of Jesus is against you.
I declare that my spiritual and natural gifts have not been violated or contaminated by any unclean spirits.
I will not be blind by any unclean spirit.
No unclean spirit will twist or pervert my thinking in the name of Jesus.
I declare that I will no longer feel emotionally and mentally raped in Jesus name.
I break off every spirit of suicide, death and destruction in Jesus name.
I break every demonic confederation associated with any unclean spirit.
Father God encamp your guardian angels around my bedpost so no unclean spirit can give me nightmares.
I repent from any and all demonic activities I'm involved in knowingly and unknowingly in Jesus name.
I command all doctrine of devils be erased from my spirit in the name of Jesus.
I break the curse of every spirit of substance abuse, sexual addictions, soul ties, deception, sodomy, mental anguish, fornication, adultery, and tainted anointing in Jesus name I'm set free.
I release a spirit of holiness, forgiveness of self, deliverance, and the fruits of the spirit over my life in Jesus name.
Father I break every vexation spirit that has come to torment me in Jesus name.
I will no longer allow demons to constantly harass me in Jesus name.
I will not give up or give in.

Call of Release

I release and call upon the Spirit of the Lord. I call forth the and release of a spirit of knowledge, counsel . . . sound mind . . . . peace . . . love of Christ . . . salvation . . . . understanding . . . wisdom . . . . fear of the Lord . . . faith . . . holiness . . . . apostolic movements . . . kingdom builders . . . region shakers . . . the heart of a mother . . . spirit of prayer . . . consecration . . . oneness in spirit . . . . spiritual understanding . . . might . . . spirit of mercy and grace . . . . forgiveness of self . . . mind of Christ . . . clarity . . . compassion . . . . favor . . . . self-acceptance . . . . fruits of the spirit . . . . dwell in the house of the Lord . . . increase . . . . money . . . and deliverance in Jesus name amen.

Daily Declaration of God Reveal To me

God reveal to me where my money is hidden.
Holy Spirit reveal to me the things of God.
Reveal to me how to be truthful with myself.
Reveal to me to hear what God is saying for our generation.
God reveal to me how to awaken my spirit to roar (Lion).
God reveal to me to see things as you see them.
Reveal to me how to release the expression of God on earth.
God reveal to me how to receive your spirit of revelation.
God reveal to me not to let anyone steal my baby and release what you have birthed in me.
Reveal to my heart how to receive your revelation.
God reveal to me the gift of love.
God reveal revelation to break the spirit of religion.
Reveal to me a deeper understanding of God's wisdom.
Reveal to me how to build a new strategy to build the church.
Reveal to me how to change my situation.
God reveal to me the inventions inside of me.
Reveal to me how to be a money magnet for the kingdom.
Reveal to me how to awaken my dreams.
God reveal to me my divine purpose.
Reveal to me how to sustain.
Reveal to me how to keep the correct mindset.
Reveal to me how to hold on to the things of God.
Reveal to me how to decree & declare a thing.
Reveal to me how to stay in your presence.
Reveal to me how to stay Holy.
Reveal to me how to hold on to your promises.
Reveal to me how to be a carrier of your Glory.
Reveal to me how to hear your voice.
Reveal to me how to enlarge my territory.
Reveal to me how to receive the glory from heaven.
Reveal to me my destiny in you.
Reveal your face to me.
Reveal to me what you need me to be.
Reveal to me how to be worshipper in truth & spirit.
Reveal your strategic plan to me.
Reveal to me how to stay spiritually hunger & stay in deliverance.
Reveal to me how to moan & groan for your presence.
Reveal to me your wondrous works.
Reveal to me how to have a grateful heart.

Daily Declaration of Expectations

I expect my spiritual mate to find me today
I expect every corporate blessing to come to pass
I expect every word true spoken over my life to come to pass
I expect to stay free from bondage
I expect the favor of God over my life, home, marriage, children, fiancés, ministry
I expect and receive the purpose of God in my life
I expect breeding ground for miracles
I expect every limitation to be broken off my mindset
I expect healing in my mind, emotions, and body,
I expect this is the day that my prophecy will come to pass
I expect to live life more abundantly
I expect to stay free from my pass and mistakes
I expect every human devil to be exposed in my path way
I expect the mouth of every negative word spoken over me to be void
I expect every assignment of satan to be cancelled off my life
I expect every hidden agenda be exposed
I expect every demonic curse written, spoken about me to be nullified
I expect my prophetic word to find its mate
I expect the thought, things, and purpose of God to be fulfilled over my life
I expect that I will not be separated from whatever God declared over my life.
I expect the lack in my life to be over
I expect the favor of God today
I expect to save the lost in this day
I expect my tongue to speak blessings not curses

Declaration for True Worship & Praise

Father God I repent from singing songs of defeat over my life
I command my praise to agitate demons & devils in the name of Jesus
The enemy will no longer be able to locate me in my praise
We will sing songs that will produce what God wants in the name of Jesus
We will create a praise that will bring reverential fear to the kingdom of darkness
Father God release an anointing of praise on every musician, and release the false musicians in the churches
Let our praise be blessed to usher us into the presence of God

We know that holiness is looking like God, may peace and favor rest on us
Let honor come to our name
Let songs of worship come from our spirits in the name of Jesus
My lips are anointed to sing, my hands are lifted to praise God
The God in me shall spring forth in the name of Jesus
My voice shall cancel the assignment of the enemy
I will not give up or give in
I'm called to change the nations with my praise
I command my spirit to reverence the spirit of God
Warfare is broken off my life when I worship
There is no limit to my praise
My worship makes war with every demonic spirit that comes against the Lamb if God
My emotions are blessed and healed by my praise
My praise has silenced the voice of darkness away from me
No devil shall come in my presence
I have access to the throne of God with my worship
As I abide in the secret place of the most high my praise shall be with me
Holy is the lamb whose blood was shed so I can praise
I welcome your presence through my worship
My worship conquers the spirit of death
My praise has delivered me from the hands of the enemy
Worship is who I am, I am a praise warrior
I will praise God all the days of my life
From this day forward my mind, will, and body shall praise the name of God
I offer my worship in spirit & truth
My praise will flow from the deepest part of me
My heart is pure before you
My worship carries me thru the storms of life
I praise because I need you
We thirst for you thank you for meeting us in worship
Father God refreshes my spirit thru praise
My praise shall move the hand of God
Every lie spoken is broken off my life thru praise.

Transformation

I believe the grace of God is sufficient for me.
I will no longer battle in my mind the things that God delivered me from.
I declare that I'm delivered from not feeling worthy God still chose me.

I have matured from every demonic attack on my life.
I will not allow satan to stop the move of God in my life.
I know who I am in Christ.
I declare that Jesus has given me present day truth.
I'm fully persuaded on who I am in Jesus.
My decision is not to stay earthbound but spiritually bound.
Heaven has made its announcement in earth concerning who I am I will bring it to manifestation.
I will move in a realm of miracles.
I will not let the vision God gave me parish.
I decree that the revelation of God has changed my mindset.
I will do the will of God while on earth.
My thought pattern will not pervert the word of God that inside of me.
I will not think in and old mindset.
I will allow the revelation of God to renew my mind and I will walk it out in Jesus name.
No revelation will stay lock in my mind.
I do not have an unrestrained mindset I have the mind of Christ in Jesus name.
I will prepare the way for my mind to be renewed.
The knowledge of God will transform me.
I will prove how good and effective the word of God is in my life.
I will not stay stuck under on revelation.
I will watch the word of God manifest in my life, my church, my region, and nation.
I will prove the will God in Jesus name.
I will speak the revelation of God on earth.
I will no longer speak ignorantly of the kingdom of God.
I will demonstrate the power and glory of God.
I am the church of God.
I will not pervert the will of God by not renewing my mind.
The present truth of God changed my mindset.
The spirit of religion will no longer make the word of God have no effect in Jesus.
I will operate as God on earth.
I declare that I am not the focus of my mentality.
I will listen and obey the voice of God.
I have the king and the kingdom inside of me.
No demonic activity is allowed to operate inside of my mind.
I know that God has cleaned me up renewed my mind so I can go back and rescue the ones that are stuck in the mess I was in.
I will advance the kingdom of God on earth.

The heart of God will make me rise into position.
The storms of life will activate what God has put inside of me.
Miracles are common to a true believer.
I declare that I have a biblical right to forget my past.

Exercising Our Authority

Father God your word tells me to use the name of Jesus as a weapon against the powers of darkness.
I submit myself wholly unto you God so that I may use your son's name.
My spirit comes into agreement that the name of Jesus shall make every demonic force take flight.
I also shall use the word of God to fight my battles and exercise my authority.
I know the power of your word it is like a two edged sword, all I need is my helmet of salvation and the sword of the spirit.
I declare that the word of God effect satan kingdom.
From this day forward I will exercise my authority by speaking the word of God over every area of my life.
Father God I also understand the power of the Holy Spirit will also guide me into using my authority.
I carry the dunamis power of the Holy Spirit within.
I will daily remind satan of the power of the blood of Jesus.
I will put into satan remembrance that he is defeated by the blood.
I understand that the blood of Jesus removes any curse and any hold the enemy had over my life.
I am an overcomer by the word of my testimony.
I will proclaim the truth where ever I go.
The truth in God will break through the powers of darkness in Jesus name amen.

Biblical Dominion

God you have given me a right to exercise my dominion here on earth.
I decree and declare that the church shall represent the authority of Christ.
I call forth every charismatic apostles and prophets in the name of Jesus.
I command every gate keeper of our city to take their posts.

I curse the Godless government and I call forth body of Christ to begin to reign and rule and take ownership of what God has given to us.

We will no longer sit around and wait for the work to be done. We will bring order to the kingdom of God.

Thank you God for doing reconstruction to the body of Christ and breaking every demonic stronghold.

I curse every hidden demon that tries to stop the dominion of God in the name of Jesus.

God I ask that you position me to fight spiritually in this season.

The grace of God will carry me in this season. No longer will I walk in defeat.

God has given us a dominion mandate to rule as God would rule.

I will walk in my ruler ship because I know who I am in Christ. I will not believe the lies of the enemy.

I repent for being a frustrated, angry, and complaining saint.

Father continue to build me on the inside so I will not become a playing field for the fiery darts of the enemy.

I curse any spirit that would attempt to keep me from understanding my dominion.

I decree that there will be unity in the body of Christ no more division, strife, envy, and jealously among the saints in Jesus name.

God I ask that you give me an increase in everything that concerns you and the ruler ship I'm anointed to walk in.

I declare this is the season for all governing churches to move. I will be sensitive to the move of God.

God we thank you for birthing new patterns for churches to become front runners for you kingdom.

I stand strong and will go through all the storms of life as a warrior for Christ.

I repent from anything I have done that will pull me away from walking in my dominion.

I have a legal right to go after what God has for me.

I will walk in a spirit of love, forgiveness, and repentance in Jesus name.

God I ask that you put more storms in my life to give me character.

I will govern my atmosphere for the kingdom of God.

I will rule in apostolic authority in my area in Jesus name.

My assignment is great the atmosphere is set for me to release the spirit of God apostolically to the nations.

God I know you want me to walk apostolically while I'm here on earth help me achieve this goal.

I grow stronger in Christ everyday there is a shifting taking place in me daily.

My warfare is about my future and those assigned to me I must push forward.

Teach me more God about walking in my dominion I realize how precious my anointing is in this hour.

Father God I break every spirit of goliath and territorial spirit in the name of Jesus.

I bind every principality that would try to stop your dominion from coming to past.

Lord guide the saints right now to walk in the full authority that is rightfully theirs.

Every spirit that tries to hinder your move I curse every hidden spirit of failure in the name of Jesus.

I take authority and dominion over every demonic force that would come against your people.

Also God I ask that you release your warring angles to wage war against all demonic activity that try to affect our minds, will and emotions.

God your word tells us that all power has been given to us in Jesus name teach us how to walk in spirit and truth in, we take back any ground that was ever lost or given to evil spirits in Jesus name I pray.

Push Me To Purpose

Lord you will accomplish that which concerns me.

Open doors that will push us into our purpose, I pray that we will receive the spirit of power that Jesus presence will be manifested in us so we can experience the fullness of God's purpose for our lives.

By the power of God we will walk into our destiny and calling.

As we walk in God's will let us be fruitful in our ministries and strengthen by intimacy with God.

We will be enriched by all the gifts of the spirit to including powerful preaching and prophetic revelation.

We need a release of God's grace to push us into purpose.

Our prayer is that we be worthy to walk in the fullness of our purpose in God.

Thankful

Father God I come to you in the name of Jesus, I thank you that from the beginning of time you already had me on your mind and predestine me for greatness.
I thank that you did not allow me to be seduced by doctrines of devils, I thank that as a child you started to teach me holiness.
I thank you above all that you taught me right from wrong; you gave me the knowledge and wisdom to know better than to be luke warm.
Your word said I can't enter into the kingdom of heaven if I'm luke warm.
I thank that you did not assign me to a church that teaches that it is ok to fornicate, it's okay to get high, that it's ok to cuss, lie steal and cheat, commit adultery, play the lotto, go on bus trips to Atlantic City.
I thank you that I'm not a homosexual trying to usher in the presence of God during praise and worship. Father right now I lift all my brothers & sister up to you who walk in spiritual blindness.
Were there pastor tells then that these things are ok have mercy on them and love them into holiness and righteousness.
The walk you put before me is not a hard work with the help of my comforter the Holy Spirit who empowers me to serve you in spirit and truth.
As my prayers go out into cyber space may they reach the one that is the closet to hell and save their souls in Jesus name AMEN.

Peace In My Spirit

Father I come to you in the name of Jesus I feel like I'm losing my mind there is so much turmoil in my home, and in my life,
Your word reassures me that I have the mind of Christ, my spirit is being pulled from every angle, I command all the fragmented parts of my spirit to return to me as one.
Father God the very ones you tell me to love unconditionally are the ones that desire my demise, I ask that you have mercy on them and forgive them just like you forgiven me.
Teach me to love unconditionally in all situations, by the power of the blood of Jesus watch over me tonight as I sleep, remove every jealous person from my life.
I know I can't give up yet my work here on earth is not finished I have souls to reach strengthen me; give me a fresh anointing to fight the human devils in my pathway.
I call on the name of Jesus to restore me, uplift, and comfort me in the name of Jesus.
As I lay down to sleep tonight encamp your guardian angels around me to minister to me were I'm wounded. I cancel the assignment of every negative and demonic word that was spoken over me in Jesus name these words are void and have no meaning. I ask these things in Jesus name AMEN

Fleshly Desires

Father God, You have told me in Romans 13:14 to put on the Lord Jesus Christ and make no provision for the flesh in regard to its lusts.
I acknowledge that I have given in to the temptation to gratify the desires of my flesh.
I understand that lust is saying, "I must have this at once."
Much of this battle is in my mind and thought life.
Because of my loneliness and inner pain at times, I have entertained lustful fantasies in my mind and thoughts.
This only increased the desire to gratify my flesh.
I ask You, Father God, reveal to me any ways in which I have broken your moral law and grieved the HolySpirit.
Father, I am truly repent for going against your word. I acknowledge that all my sins are forgiven in Christ.

I claim the blood of Jesus over me as my protection.
I come before your presence to acknowledge these sins that I might be freed from the bondage of sin. I now confess these sins to you and claim through the blood of the Lord Jesus Christ my forgiveness and cleansing.
I repent and cancel all access to my life that evil spirits have gained through my willful involvement in sin.
I claim the blood of Jesus over me as my protection and command them to leave me now in Jesus' name.
I choose to walk by the guidance of the Holy Spirit, in Jesus' name. Amen

Sinners Prayer

Father God in the name of Jesus I repent from all my sins and invite you into my heart & life as my personal savior. I believe that Jesus died on the cross for my sins please forgive me of my sins I have committed. Right now I confess Jesus as the Lord of my soul. This very moment I accept Jesus Christ as my own personal Savior and according to His Word, right now I am saved.
Therefore Lord Jesus transform my life so that I may bring glory and honor to you alone and not to myself. Thank you Jesus for dying for me and giving me eternal life.
Your word says in Romans 10:9 That if thou shalt confess with thy mouth the Lord Jesus, and shalt believe in thine heart that God hath raised him from the dead, thou shalt be saved.

The Hand Of God

This was in my spirit as soon as I awoke this morning. When I cry or when I hurt where are you, when the flood comes against me you said you would lift a standard and protect me, when the words from another pierce my soul and cut like a knife where were you, when I sat alone and did not know the words to say, when the inside of me was crying and I felt no relief where were you, Then God you took my mind to a place that gave me peace in this vision was your hand that held my heart, your hand pulled the knife out of my heart, then I saw the mighty hand of God fighting all my battles and that is why I can say The mighty Hand of God kept me when I couldn't keep myself, kept my mind in perfect peace, God all I can say is continue to stretch out your hand over my life and everything that concerns me in Jesus name amen.

Unsaved Loved Ones

Lord Jesus Christ, I stand in the gap for (name), and counter-petition for their soul and spirit in Your Name, Lord. I plead the Blood between them and Satan and every evil spirit and work of darkness. I pray a hedge of protection around them to keep them from the wiles of the enemy. By faith in Jesus' name, Father, I dispatch warrior angels and ministering angels to go forth immediately to minister to (name), to protect him/her, to turn the enemy back and drive the enemy out of their life, to retrieve soul-fragments by force, which I call restored to (name) and re-integrated into their soul-life by Your Spirit of power and might of the Holy Spirit.
Father, Jesus said that no man can come to Him unless called by the Father. Please, Father, have compassion upon (name). Call them to Jesus give them the desires and grace to respond and reach out, that they may have a revelation of who Jesus is. Where there is a heart of stone give them a heart of flesh, soften their hearts to receive your word and salvation. Show them your mercy and your grace and make a way out for them. Make them to see with the eyes of your spirit and give them your ears to hear from your spirit. Do not withhold any good thing Jesus so they will know it is an encounter from you. God you promised that me and my household would be saved and I believe in your word. Perform you word over their lives in Jesus name amen.

Prayer for Forgiveness

Father, in Christ Jesus' Name, I lay down at your feet all present and past unforgiveness, anger, bitterness, or resentment, directed at (name or names). I repent of it and renounce it all, and ask you to forgive me for it. I forgive and release them. I repent for anyone who was hurt by it, and ask for your forgiveness for that also. I forgive and release myself of all unforgiveness, anger, resentment and bitterness also. I renounce this and all past sin, and ask you to forgive me, Lord Jesus Christ. I ask all these things in Your Holy Name, Amen."

Prayer to set free

In the name of Jesus, I cut satan, his demons and curses loose from me, my family and friends. I command you, satan, and all evil spirits and curses to

loose me and my family and all the things you have stolen from us (happy marriages, finances, jobs, families, ministries, health, etc.).
I command you to stop robbing us of our blessings and blocking God's perfect will for our lives. I refuse to allow you to steal anything else's from us.
I command you to lose all natural resources, land, animals, money, the finances of people who owe us money, and all the things you have stolen from us that are ours through the blessings of Jesus. I ask you, Lord, to send your angels to bring these things back to us. In Jesus' name, Amen."

Prayer Against Suicide

I now come before your throne in the name of my Lord and Savior Jesus Christ. I believe that demons have now come in on me with the compulsions and thoughts of suicide that I am now having. These demons are trying to get me to take my own life, but am not going to fall for their evil deception Father, in the name of Jesus, I now want to take a firm and final stand against these demons and get them off me once and for all. Per the review of my life for all of the possible things that may have been door openers for these demons to be able to come in and attach themselves to me—I now come before You to once and for all break any legal rights these demons may be operating on with me.
Amen

Daily Temptations

Dear Lord. You know the temptations that I am facing today. But your Word promises that I will not be tempted beyond what I can bear. I ask for your strength to stand up under the temptation whenever I encounter it. Your Word also tells me you will provide a way out of the temptation. Please, Lord, give me the wisdom to walk away when I am tempted, and the clarity to see the way out that you will provide. Thank you, God, that you are a faithful deliverer and that I can count on your help in my time of need. Help me fight the enemy that is too strong for me to bear. I need your help to make it through what I'm facing. God I tired of sinning against you, I cry out for your help. I know right from wrong but I always choose wrong. Help me to die to my flesh and my selfish desires. This day I choose life not death. Raise a standard against the enemy in my life right know the enemy knows me just like you do God, this temptation looks too good to pass, give me the strength to leave the bondage of this world. Deception is all around me, help me right know in Jesus name I pray Amen

Return to What

You have life and life more abundantly. So why are you looking back wanting to give up. What's there to go back to . . . NOTHING . . . satan is hot on our tails that is his job to distract, discourage, and bring confusion. I command the mind of Christ be downloaded into you, I command your spirit to line of to the word of God . . . Amen

I hear the spirit of the Lord saying I have mend all the breaks and tears in your heart with the blood of my son Jesus, the tears you cry are cleansing tears that my angels bottle up in heaven, your tears mean allot to me. Go through this season and stand strong my child for my hand is with you. I'm searching your heart and removing all infections (people) that I don't want in your path or life. Don't force or hold on to what I'm removing no matter what the relationship is to you let go of them. I will not leave a void or a gap in your life . . . sayeth the Lord . . . . Amen

God told the devil I know _____ drinks, gets high, in an adulteress relationship, lies, steals, cheats, walks around angry and confused, very dysfunctional. But I'm going to use _____ anyway. I spoke into their life when I created the heavens and the earth; I made plans for them when death wanted them. I created _____ to be victorious, mighty. God said he is not looking at the outward appearance; I look at the inward parts of my children.

You don't ask the devil nothing you have the authority and advantage over him. Don't get discouraged when the devil comes against you he comes to discourage you. That is his full time job. He wants you to be confused to stop what God spoke over your life. The devil wants you to speak negativity and defeat over your life. You strengthen the devils plans when you speak against yourself. If the devil has a full time job why are we part time Christians?

You wipe your prayers out of the heavenlies when you speak against what you just prayed for the power of life and death is in the tongue. Think before you speak no matter what it looks like God has the final say.

If you pray bold prayers, God will do bold things in your life. What are you praying boldly for?and you have to believe that you will get what you ask for in faith. There is nothing to big or small to ask our God for.

Stop running from the past. Simply make a decision to face it and receive your healing. If there is anything in your past that is good for you God will bring it to you don't go searching yourself.

When you run wild he loves it, when you cry he laughs, when you don't learn from your mistakes, he gets joy, when your emotions go up & down like a roller coaster, he has you. The devil comes to steal, kill & destroy, why make it easier for him to attack you.

You are My offspring, says the Lord. You belong to Me. The past days, months, or even years of struggle are becoming a thing of the past as I prepare you for this time of new things. Refuse to allow the fears, disappointments and failures of the past to dictate your current course. Allow Me to bring forth a transformation. I will heal the brokenness of the past and give you new hope for the future.

Jeremiah 29:11 For I know the thoughts that I think toward you, says the LORD, thoughts of peace and not of evil, to give you a future and a hope.

When God mends your broken heart it is your faith that helps you through. His blood mends and heals the scars, he whispers to your spirit and you are fresh and anew, the angels encamp around you. His covering protects you, God knows all the plans for your life so why go off course because of pain & failure. It is at that point when character is build inside of you. Let go of the past and grab onto God's future.

Your destiny is not cancelled because of a mistake, because of a failure. Get right with God and those that may have been hurt and keep it moving!!

Your presence is a present to the world. You are unique and one of a kind. Do not ever forget, for even a day how very special you are! Remember you are the salt of the earth, the flavor to the world!

Without confrontation of painful issues from the past, it is impossible to go forward with a healthy soul. Beyond feelings deal with your past before your past deals with you. What's to be ashamed of God forgave you blessed you and changed you.

God wants to get you to your future your destiny. Have you felt that you have been through so much that you can't take it anymore. You are a bow & arrow and God is pulling the bow to the point that you can't take it. You cry, pray, wonder is it worth it. The golden part is when God lets go and shoots you into your purpose. When you arrive on the other side purpose start asking God for the things he has for you. Remember you are a designer original there is no other like you in his creation.

Instead of branches Jesus removed tree's from my life and that was a hurt piece . . . but it was all for the glory of God. Sometime we try to hold on to the things that we are so use to and comfortable with. I learned the hard way if you are going to trust God let him take the lead.

When I cry or when I hurt where are you, when the flood comes against me you said you would lift a standard and protect me, when the words from another pierce my soul and cut like a knife where were you, when I sat alone and did not know the words to say, when the inside of me was crying and I felt no relief where were you, Then God you took my mind to a place that gave me peace in this vision was your hand that held my heart, your hand pulled the knife out of my heart, then I saw the might hand of God fighting all my battles and that is why I can say The mighty Hand of God kept me when I couldn't keep myself, kept my mind in perfect peace. God all I can say is continue to stretch out your hand.

We need to thank God for the backstabbers, the ones who gossip about you, tell lies, just hate for no reason, envy you, want to be in your shoes, I thank you for all the false rumors you spread, "Thank you for the advertisement about my life" you advertised me so much people want to see who I really am, what I am really about!

You're about to get your bounce back. "The enemy strategically plotted against you, hunted you like prey, set out to destroy you, tried to wreck your mind, destroy your heart, jack up your family, take your ministry, ruin your reputation . . . and he thought that he had you. He set you up and thought this is what will kill them. "I came to put every devil on notice . . . I'm getting my dream back, I'm getting my prophesy back, I'm getting my vision back, I'm getting my anointing back, I'm getting my strength back."

Today I can say thank you to God for when I was in sin he still loved me and not the sin, when I couldn't love myself he still loved me. When I was in a world of darkness he became the light in my life, when I tried to kill myself death wanted me but God wanted me more. Thank you God for the peace and the mind of Christ.

I Decree That Death Is the Gift Of A Finisher

I declare that I do not have a fear of death.
When God is done with me in the earthly realm the gift of eternity will be given unto me.
I declare that God has not put any sickness on my body.
I serve notice to the spirit of death that you do not have any rights or grounds to take me out.
I declare that I discover what my assignment on earth is and I will carry it out to the finish.
God I thank you that your mercy stopped me from getting what I deserved when I was in the world and that your grace gave me what I didn't deserve.
I thank you for hiding me in the secret place of the most high.

I will not entertain no thoughts of death in the name of Jesus I have not made an appointment with death.
Until my assignment is done devil I'm right here on earth destroying the kingdom of darkness.
I declare I will not help the spirit of death come upon me.
I declare that in my own flesh I cannot carry what God said he has already taken care of.
I will give all my cares over to God. No devil can take my life I lay down my life.
I will enjoy my life in Jesus I serve God because I love him.
My healing comes through my laughter.
I realize that death is an evaluation of my completion.
Teach me to number my day's thank you for another day in Jesus name amen.

Daily Declaration

You are my healer.
You are my provider.
You are my deliver.
You are who I trust.
God is on my side.
God will never leave me or forsake me.
God is always with me.
The spirit of God helps me live a life of purity.
You are my glory.
I receive your confidence.
You daily load me with benefits.
I can do all things through Christ who strengthen me.
God is my judge.
God carries me through the storms of life.
I daily receive from the Holy Spirit.
God is my hope.
I have the gift of eternal life.
I am free in the spirit.
I receive the revelation of the Lord.
Nothing can keep me from the love of God.
All my hindrances are removed by the blood of Jesus.
I will allow the Holy Spirit to keep order in my life.
I'm never alone.
My nourishment begins with the word of God.
I am the righteousness of Christ Jesus.

A Prophetic Release of the Four Winds

Father God I call a release of the East Wind in the name of Jesus.
I call forth the judgment of the east wind to curse and destroy every demonic confederacy.
I declare that there will be judgment to every false apostle, prophet, minister, and elder that the east wind will expose and tear down every demonic altar in the name of Jesus.
Let the winds blow with great power and force.
Father God every time we speak of the east wind let it bring judgment of God.
I release the power and might of the four winds.
I release the spiritual effects of each wind of God upon the land in the name of Jesus.
I declare that when the east wind blows it will deal with witches and warlocks in our region.
Father God I ask that you visit every witch and warlock and save their souls.
I release the east wind to break and destroy all demonic principalities in the name of Jesus.
Release your wind to remove everything that is not like God in our lives.
After the apostolic winds are released bring healing, freedom, restoration, and salvation to our land.

I call forth a release of the South wind to bring provision to your people in the name of Jesus.
I release abundance and more than enough in lives.
Release provision to carry out every prophetic and apostolic vision that God has given us.
Let the south winds release a higher anointing from the Holy Spirit.
I decree that the power of God will make changes in this season.
I declare that the south wind is my provision from God.

I call forth a release of the North wind in the name of Jesus.
The north wind shall blow in the presence of God.
I shall receive my refreshing with the rain from the north wind.
I call forth a revival to be released, a fresh anointing from the winds of God.
The north wind shall bring to past the spoken word of God.
I release the north wind to water my seed in the name of Jesus.
The north wind will release a fresh move of God.
Every blessing that God has for me will be released when the north wind blows.
I release the north winds to take away evil and release the good in Jesus name.

I call forth a release of the West Wind to remove all hindrances in my life in Jesus name.
The west wind will stop every demonic force trying to stop the move of God in my life.
I release the west wind to break every stronghold in my life, region, nation, city and church in the name of Jesus.
I will allow the west winds to expose the hidden things in my life.
The west wind will also bring great deliverance to my life and my unsaved family in Jesus name.
I pray that the west wind be release over the United States of America.

God in Me

God show me the God that is in me.
Reveal to me the gifts I have inside of me.
Holy Spirit also reveal the hidden things of God inside of me.
I have a full grown Jesus on the inside of me.
I decree this is the hour to be truthful with myself.
I will open my ears spiritual and hear what God has to say about me and my generation.
In this season God is pouring out his spirits on all.
I will receive a rich amount of Gods spirit for me.
Father God I ask that you awaken the lion on the inside of me, give me a roar that will bring salvation and deliverance to everyone in my path way.
I will see things as God see things.
We desire the expression of God on earth.
It is time for me to stand in my anointing.
I'm no longer a punk in the spirit.
Let the true prophets of the land activate the voice of God in others.
Father God release your spirit of revelation upon my life.
God I ask that you anoint my eyes that I will be able to see in the spirit.
God touch my ears to hear in the spiritual realm.
My spirit is awaken by the power of God.
I realize that I'm about to give birth in the spiritual realm and nobody but God will name my baby.
Give me a heart to receive your revelation; I want the heart of God.
I know all God's gift work through the spirit of love.
God has put inside of me a spirit to break religion, understanding, and the wisdom of God.
God give me a new strategy to rebuild your church.

The revelation of God will change my situation.
My new revelation will bring forth new inventions for the kingdom of God.
God please awaken my dreams that lay dormant inside of me.
God reveal my divine purpose.

Prophetic Me

Father God in Jesus name I thank you that you want to reveal to me through your spirit.
I understand that you want to give me deep understanding of the deep things of God.
From this day forward I will not tap illegally into the spiritual realm I will tap into the spiritual realm through God.
God I understand your will for my life everything was freely given to me by the work that was done on the cross.
I decree that I will not allow my heart to look for answers that God has already given to me.
I stand and believe the word of God if God spoke it I don't need a co-signer.
I don't want anything in my life that is against the will of God for me. I will no longer be bound.
I repent for praying the famous "If it is your will".
I decree that religion will not rob me to believe that God put any kind of sickness on my body due to disobedience.
Jesus said "Let your will be done". Jesus said my flesh will not receive the will of God.
Thank you heavenly father for dealing with my spirit.
I praise God knowing his holy word will agitate my spirit.
The conviction of the Holy Spirit will not allow me to walk any old way instead it will keep me in a place to always hear from the Holy Spirit.
I repent from allowing my flesh to think for me in the name of Jesus.
I will no longer feed my flesh this will desensitize me further away from Gods will for my life.
I will not listen to the voices for people when I go through a storm.
I will stay in the presence of God and he will guide me through my storm.
I decree that prophetic people hear and understand the voice and council of Gods mind.
God will always give me what he is thinking and what he wants done in the earthly realm.
In Jesus name I will not allow my spirit to shift so I can't hear from God.

I can go before God and ask all questions that are on my heart I will not allow the spirit of religion to tell me I cannot.
God is trying to get something to me and I'm ready to receive.
I must understand what God is saying.
I will only connect with people who walk in the council of God.
Father God open my ears to hear clearly in this hour.
I will support the ministry of the apostles, and prophets in the church.
I'm able to speak and spring forth the rhema word revealing the mind and purpose of God.
I decree that I will legislate on behalf of heaven.
I earnestly desire spiritual gifts and I will use them.
I heard heavens promise and it will come to past what was spoken over my life and my family's life.
I decree that I'm not standing on what I see but I'm standing on what God said.
I repent from having a low self-esteem and a religious spirit in Jesus name I am the righteousness of God.
I decree that it takes the Holy Spirit to keep me pure I have yield my spirit over.
My past is my past God don't remember it why should I. I'm delivered from my past.
I decree that I will incorporate scriptures in my prayers.
It's a honor to have the Holy Spirit live inside of me.
If I don't faint I'm going to reap the blessing of the Lord are mine.
Father God thank you for all the times you interceded for me.
I will not cause unnecessary pain in my life.
I will no longer pray selfish prayers in the name of Jesus.
I will stop saying that God favors other people more than me.
God even when I can't trace you I'm still trusting in you.
I decree that God is my source not my job.
God I will rest my spirit and operate out of the spirit of God.
I will cast my cares upon God so my spirit will not be sluggish.
My spirit is prophetic so I can worship God.

My Children

Father God in Jesus name I decree that my children shall be what you called them to be.
I declare my children are blessed and highly favored.
My children shall live and not die.
The hand of God is upon my seed.
My children shall not live in not enough they will instead live in the overflow.
I command an overflow of the spirit of God to reach my child in Jesus name.
I call forth my child's salvation in the name of Jesus my seed shall preach and teach the word of God.
From this day forward my child will no longer have anything to do with powers of darkness.
As the blood of Jesus covers my child they will fear no evil in Jesus name.
I cancel the assignment of destruction, death, vagabond, confusion, lust, lying, pharmeka, alcohol, doctrine of devils, idolatry, sexual sins, deaf and dumb spirits, spiritual blindness, homosexuality, lesbian, false worship, religion, poverty, anger, bitterness, I command these spirits and every cousin spirit to leave my Childs life and to never return. I command you to the pits of hell in Jesus name.

I thank you father that my child will not lose their mind while taking any drugs.
I break the assignment of the drug ritalin, embalming fluid, wet, ecstasy, reefer in the name of Jesus.
Satan I command you to lose my child now in the name of Jesus.
I decree that the gates of hell will not prevail against my child's life in Jesus name.
I bind up every principality, ruler of darkness, evil spirits, and all familiar spirits from operating in my childs life.
I bind every assignment against my children in the name of Jesus.
I say that every familiar spirit from this day forward will no longer be able to follow my child.
I cancel every ungodly prayer that was prayed over my seed in the name of Jesus.
I release a spirit of holiness over my child.
By the grace of God my child shall complete high school, go to college, have successful careers, be a home owner, my child will stay pure for the one God has assigned to be their mate.
Every hindering spirit must leave now in the name of Jesus.

I declare that my child shall reign in life.
I declare that my child will not be a failure in life my child has purpose.
I break the assignment of all negativity off of my child in the name of Jesus.
I declare that every stubborn, hidden, demon and every stronghold is broken off my seed in the name of Jesus.
I cancel every satanic and demonic claim over my child's life in the name of Jesus.
My child shall represent the glory of God.

Spirit of Sheba

I decree that I will not go against the man or women of God and I will not cause confusion in my church.
I renounce a know it all attitude in the name of Jesus.
I need to connect to people in my church.
I have a mindset that requires me to go forward in the kingdom of God.
I understand my covenant with God. No devil in hell will come between my covenant.
I declare that I have no hidden agenda in Jesus name.
God sent me to the church to be developed not come against leadership.
I will not allow my life to be a base for the spirit of Sheba to operate from.
I will not fall under the spirit of suspicion, and distrust in Jesus name.
The enemy will not take my imagination where it does not belong.
I will not allow the spirit of Sheba to attack my marriage or my anointing.
The spirit of Sheba will never tell me I don't belong to my local assembly.
I silence the voice of the spirit of Sheba from whispering to me while I'm at church in Jesus name.
I decree that backsliding is not an option for me.
Satan I serve you notice no matter what comes my way I'm not turning back.
I will allow God to do a divine separation.
I command the spirit of Sheba to leave every congregation in my city region and nation in Jesus name.
I will not allow this spirit to break unity in my church.
I know that it is dangerous to operate under this spirit in Jesus name.
I decree that I will not help leaders tear down the walls of distrust in Jesus name.
I curse the spirit of Sheba from making mindset believe that if they won't do in the church it will not get done.
I decree that I am not the only one in my church who can sing, preach, and teach in Jesus name.
I release a spirit of unity upon my church the spirit of Sheba hates unity.
I decree that as soon as I come into full maturity the spirit of Sheba will come to oppose my unity with my church.
I declare that the spirit of Sheba will not stop me from seeing the vision, or the corporate destiny that surrounds me in Jesus name.
I cancel the power of Sheba to bring instability, confusion to the body of Christ.
I decree that if your name is involved in all the trouble at your church you are carrying a spirit of Sheba.

I will not allow the spirit of Sheba to stop me from going to bible study, church, and prayer in Jesus name.
I decree that the spirit of Sheba will come to magnify any trouble in the church.
I decree that I will not allow the spirit of Sheba to give me a mindset that the leaders are doing what they are supposed to in Jesus name.
I declare that the spirit of Sheba gets energy off of atmosphere of strife, and disunity.
I curse the spirit of Sheba from keeping the saints from fellowshipping, and not to recognize the gifts that are inside of you. Trying to disconnect you from the corporate vision, trying to mess up the move of God in Jesus name.
In Jesus name I understand my spiritual authority and can deal with the spirit of Sheba
I declare that I have been birthed into apostolic mindset and I walk in my kingdom authority in Jesus name.
I decree that I will learn to walk in the spirit that my countenance will not show that I am going through.

Being Obedient to the Heavenly Vision

The warfare in my mind is for the vision of the people of the world.
I agree with the vision of my church.
I will not allow the devil to disconnect me I decree this in the name of Jesus.
The devil cannot stop me mentally, physically, nor can he stop the vision inside of me.
I declare that I will be an obedient servant of God.
God I realize that the people who talk about me is all part of your plan for my life.
I will not give in to my weakness and I will not allow anyone to use my weakness as a weapon against me.
I will walk in true holiness to complete the vision of God.
I decree that no one can control me with their resources in Jesus name.
I see it with my spiritual eye and believe it with my natural eye.
I will bring into reality what I see spiritually.
The devil knows that me and my seed will do damage to his kingdom.
I will being to walk out what I see in the heavenlies.
What God has given me will be in my linage.
My encounter with Jesus is what opens my eyes to see.
I will not deny what I am connected to.

I'm affected by the prophetic it's called Jesus is contagious.
My vision is a driving force in the kingdom this is where God says I'm going.
I will implement mission to bring my vision to pass.
I am like Isaac a promised seed.

I'm Free

I'm free from every ungodly soul tie that had me bound.
I'm free from the grips of the enemy.
I'm free of my past and present mistakes.
My mind is free in Christ.
I free from a low self-esteem.
I'm free from depression and oppression in Jesus name.
I free from the bondage of mankind.
I'm free from every demonic trap.
I'm free of every spoken curse spoken about me.
I'm free from the snare of the enemy.
I'm free from the spirit of lust.
I'm free from bad memories.
I'm free of the hurt from the past.
I'm free of my guilt from my past.
I'm free from other people's opinion.
I'm free from a cursed tongue.
I'm free from a demonic mind set.
I'm free indeed.
I'm free from drugs and alcohol.
I'm free from lying.
I'm free from all sexual sins.
I'm free from a judgmental mindset.
I'm free from the warfare in my mind.
I'm free from not knowing.
I'm free from demonic activity taking place in my life.
I'm free from jealousy, envy, and bitterness.
I'm free from other people's emotions.
I'm free from every hindering spirit.
I'm free from spiritual blindness.
I'm free from a broken heart.
I'm free from a broken spirit.
I'm free of not being loved and wanted.

I'm free of my divorce.
I'm free from the judgment of witchcraft.
I'm free from all black magic, spells, and incantations.
I'm free from every trap and snare of the devil.
I'm free from the gates of hell.
I'm free from all curses, hexes, vexes, bewitchments, and enchantments.
I'm free from the demonic realm locating me in Jesus name.
I'm free from all voodoo, sorcery, blood pacts, blood sacrifices, blood covenants, animal sacrifices, and all occult practices of any kind.
I'm free from the sins of my ancestors, and every generational curse.
I'm free from vain thoughts and imaginations.
I'm free from mind control in Jesus name.
I'm free from doubt and all anxieties.
I'm free from all physics assignments against me.
I'm free from my inner pain.
I'm free from lack and not enough.
I'm free from spiritual stagnation.
I'm free from all demonic and satanic activities.
I'm free from any appointment with death in Jesus name Amen.

I'm Not Looking Back

I know how God moves in my life.
My heart will always stay connected to Gods heart.
This is my season to recognize the timing of God and his movement.
God has sent us what we need apostolically and prophetically for his kingdom.
I decree I will not look back and ask myself go back to what.
I decree I will take the time to stay in God's presence.
This is my season for divine alignment in Jesus name.
I will no longer wrestle with the spirit of God.
God is going to move in the inconvenient part of my life.
I recognize the visitation from the Holy Spirit.
My daily life activities will no longer distract me from the move of God.
I will give my most precious to God.
I willing to see Gods glory in my present day.
I rebuke every spirit of dullness in Jesus name.
I see the revelation and will of God.
My heart is not far from God.
I bear witness to the hang of God moving like never before.

I decree that I have reverential fear of the Lord.
I will respond to all miracles.
I curse every wicked spirit released against the earth in Jesus name.
Thank you God for moving the mockery off of the church.
God is going to shut the mouths of those that laughed at me.
God is coming after the precious the first in your life.
I'm stepping into the threshold of change.
I decree that I will no longer linger behind.
I will stop lingering in what God is judging.
No hesitation will stop my destiny in God.
I repent from having a lingering and hesitant spirit in Jesus name.
I will eat from the tree of life.
Thank you God for release me from the ties in my life.
My provision is waiting in the place of my next assignment.
Alignment is my assignment.
I will not put new wine into old wine skins in Jesus name.
I will move because the heavens are open.
I release stability on the body of Christ.
I meditate on things that are true.
I have a heart to perceive.
God will make everything hidden come to life when he shows up in my life.
Vision will make me focus.
God is moving by his judgments and blessings.
I curse every Pharaoh spirit in the name of Jesus.
The way I live my life will change my city.
I declare this to be a season of humility in the body of Christ.
I'm connected to the move of God.
I'm the salt of the earth.
I rebuke every spirit of indifference in me in Jesus name.
I decree that God moves on my desires I have an opinion.
I will not miss the move of God by being passive.
I have favor with God and man to accomplish kingdom work.
My DNA looks like my father God.
I decree that fear will not paralyze me in Jesus name.
I decree I won't look back when Jesus starts to move in my life.
I will let go of my own maturity in Jesus name.
I don't remember the former things and I don't consider the things of old.
I decree that the voice of the Lord is full of majesty and power.
I decree that God has highlighted things in my heart and I shall spring forth.
I decree that God is releasing his supernatural favor, and power.
My obedience is what defines me in Jesus name.

I Speak To My Mind

I speak to my mind I declare you are renewed.
I curse every demonic pattern that illegally enters my thought life.
I speak to the Jesus in my mind while he downloads his thoughts and plans for me.
Every stronghold that lived in my mind I command you to the pits of hell.
I release a fresh anointing in my mind. I release a kingdom mindset that will speak apostolically to every situation in my life.
I no longer listen or obey the voice of the enemy.
My mind shall be free and occupied by the Holy Spirit the rest of my days in Jesus name.
I declare every fragmented part of my mind is restored one hundred percent.
The blood of Jesus stops every curse on my mind.
I declare that my mind has been made whole.
I speak to my mind and command it to forget the past right now in Jesus name.
The fire of God has been released in my mind to burn up every barren place and idol thoughts in Jesus name.
I decree that no longer will spirit of distraction occupy my mind.
I call forth the stability of my mind in Jesus name.
My mind has lined up with the mind of Christ.
Peace I speak to my mind.
The hand of God has transformed my mind to receive present day truth in Jesus name.
I declare that my mind will no longer run wild my mind will not linger behind.
Who the son has set free is free indeed.

Second Wind of My Destiny

That you God for breathing on me taking me from dimension to dimension.
The wind of my destiny takes me to another level in Christ.
I live for the second wind to blow on my life.
I decree that I anticipate the great things to come.
I'm positioning myself for something wonderful.
The things of my yesterday have passed away.
I decree that all the new is coming to me in Jesus name.

I'm not going to walk in my yesterday I'm expecting the new.
I decree that manifestation will bring miracles into my life.
I know God will make it happen for me.
I'm no longer running on empty.
I call forth the Rachel in me.
I declare that I hear the sound of the wind blowing in my life.
An overflow of newness is upon me.
The new wind will give me a sense of purpose.
I just don't exist I know why I'm here.
I decree that the wind is going to set me in God's vein.
I'm a spiritual being in Christ.
I decree that once I tap into the flow of God's vein I will never be broke, miserable, confused, in poverty, depressed, or ashamed of whom I am.
I decree that God will breathe life into that which is dead inside of me.
I will never forget God, God will sew fulfillment into my life.
I receive daily his breath of freshness into my life in Jesus name.
God will continue to breathe on me to release the prophetic wind in me.
I declare that the same places I lost the battle I'm going back to win the war in Jesus name.
I decree that God is doing something over in my life the same place the devil stepped on.
Satan is defeated with the wind that is blowing.
When the enemy wanted me to give up God gave me a new sound, a new worship, a new dimension in him.
I decree the wind of God has birth the righteousness of God in me.
I decree that I'm going to keep on keeping on until I prevail and my promises come to pass, my purpose and destiny.
My second wind brought life to me a new birthing I have an appointment with God.
Don't count me out I have a tremendous comeback in Jesus name.
I decree that I have hidden ammunition inside of me.
The second wind is coming in a greater force.
It's confirmed I am God on earth his likeness and image.
My purpose is tied to hundreds of souls for the kingdom of God.
I decree that I don't have to mention the things in my past it's a done deal that door is closed and sealed by the blood of Jesus.
I decree that I won't go back to the whispers of my past.
The words of God will not pass me by.
I decree that my past is "Ashes to ashes dust to dust".
I cancel every mark of wickedness on my life in Jesus name.
I decree that destiny is calling my name I must connect.
I feel the thrust of God's wind.

I decree that God is using the second wind to uncover my greatness, my hidden treasures, and my potential.
My hardships brought out the life in me.
I'm on my way to a place "THIS".
God wants me to rest in the reality of what he spoke over my life what has already been established in the heavenlies.
I decree that I am a "GLORY CARRIER" there are nations in me.
I decree that I got a river of life flowing out of me in Jesus name.
I'm in my season of my satisfaction Jesus is the satisfaction of my soul.
I decree that all restriction are off of my life in Jesus name.
God gave me beauty for the ashes he blew away.
I don't remember my ashes the painful place, the reality of what happen to me, it was not the truth about me.
I decree that God represents the center of my heart.
I decree that I will bring grace to people.
God blows from the place of restriction.
I decree that I hear the winds of a new assignment.
I will walk in boldness, confidence, and a new anointing.
God gave me the anointing to flourish and to produce in Jesus name.
I decree that God is trying to get heaven to me so I can do heaven on earth.
God blew in the secret places to remove my demons, the sin no one knows about, the lies, and deception. The areas that are weak that the devil comes in at.
I decree that God blew into to me the sword of perseverance in Jesus name.
I failed in the first wind.
God wrapped up eternity in me.
I decree it's time for me to change my perception in Jesus name.

God Given Direction

Jesus I understand that you need our faith to manifest the promises of God.
Jesus you are welcomed to have your kingdom back.
I declare there will be a corporate spirit of faith in the body of Christ.
I thank you God that in a corporate unity of faith no one needs to preach.
I'm going to carry the burden of someone else in Jesus name.
I declare that there is a oneness in the spirit.
I decree my steps are ordered by the word of God.
I declare I'm not going to focus on what I don't like about someone there are things that God don't like about me.

I will not count someone's anointing out because of something they have done. I will focus on the man in the mirror.

I declare that where there is a corporate anointing there can be a manifestation of a corporate anointing.

God wants us to feel him in the spirit.

My anointing don't work among anointed people it works in region where there is witchcraft, on my job, unbelief, and a religious region.

I declare that the pull of the anointing goes deeper than an individual.

I declare I will get my emotions out of the way and let God move.

We are a people that are ready for the battle.

I will allow God to download daily in my life.

Thank you god for hand picking mighty men and women of God.

I declare that God is going to respond to the hunger of his people.

I decree that one word can destroy a legion of demons in our city.

We must raise up the standard over our cities and regions in Jesus name.

God display a mirror for the world to show what is ungodly.

I decree that I will not allow satan to shut me up from what I believe.

Because I'm holding on God is going to give me victory in Jesus name.

When my flesh is fighting what Go is doing in my life that is the greatest breakthrough.

I decree that I will not give up what I'm doing I don't want my prayers and fasting to be in vain.

I decree that I will be able to withstand what others go through.

I decree that in the end I will still be standing.

The battle that I am facing is the heritage of a nation, city and region.

I must stand the ground for the battle that is ahead of me.

Clarion Call of God's People

I decree that I accept the clarion call from God in Jesus name.
I declare that my spirit heard the sound to walk in true holiness.
My ears are open to hear from God.
The clarion call will help me walk in grace and knowledge in Jesus name.
The clarion call will release the trump of God on earth.
The trumpet of grace is highly received in an apostolic atmosphere.
The clarion call will restore the kingdom of God on earth.
I decree that the devil is mad that I heard the clarion call in the spirit and received it in Jesus name.
God I ask that you open the ears of the saints of God so they can hear the clarion call and obey their calling.
I thank you that spiritual warfare is done when the kingdom worshippers receive the clarion call.
I decree that demonic principalities are broken over cities, region, and nation when the clarion call is released.
The clarion call breaks all religious spirits in Jesus name.
I declare that the adversary will not stop the kingdom of God from hearing the clarion call.
Due to the clarion call every strategy of the enemy is exposed and defeated in Jesus name.
Satan I serve you notice that you can no longer stop the clarion call from being heard.
Father God I ask that you fine tune my hearing to the clarion call.
I will be obedient to the call of God.
I declare that the clarion call of God will expose my hidden sin.
The clarion call will give me a testimony for Christ.
The clarion call will help me resist and recognize the schemes and plans of the enemy against my life.
I will use the clarion call for spiritual vigilance.
I decree that the clarion call will help me be a watchman in the spirit.
I will not leave my post in Jesus name.
I decree that the clarion call will lead me to repentance.
The clarion call will bring transformation to my mind and spirit in Jesus name.
The clarion call will wake up the lazy ones in the kingdom.
I decree that the clarion call will release the treasures of God.
Those that hear the clarion call will labor for Christ.
God let the clarion call expose all doctrines of devils in Jesus name.
The clarion call is preparation to a higher anointing a new flow in Jesus.

I Decree My Billions

I decree that money shall come to me in large amounts in the name of Jesus.
I decree that God will release his heavenly angels to go and unearth and uncover all my missed blessings, and money that is mine.
I am the head and not the tail the lender not the borrower.
I decree that by faith I see myself as a billionaire in Jesus name.
My over flow is to advance the kingdom of God.
I decree that my hearts desires will come to pass and God is my source for provision.
I command money to come out of the hands of the wicked and come to me in Jesus name.
The word of God speaks to me about wealth, money and riches.
I am a money magnet everywhere I go money comes to me.
I decree that my billions will bless my generation and the next generation to come in Jesus name.
I command every entrepreneur spirit to be stirred up in me, every business plan, and every investment shall also be stirred up in me.
I walk in the abundance of Gods riches.
God's divine purpose is for me and my family to be blessed.
I decree that I have a anointing for wealth and prosperity.
I decree that all debt under my name and children's name has been cancelled.
My name is the favor of God.
I shall bless the poor and weak, I shall feed and clothe the homeless, I shall build houses, christian schools, colleges, and I shall own the first all Christian football/basketball/baseball teams, I shall own christian day care centers, I shall own recovery houses worldwide, I shall own hospitals, I shall own gospel radio and TV station worldwide, I shall my own publishing company, I shall own my own restaurants, I shall own my own oil wells, I shall own my own Jewelry Store, I shall own Wall Street. The government will come to me to borrow, I shall my own chain of banks, and credit unions, I shall own a clothing line, I shall own coffee house, I shall own an insurance company, I shall own my own movie studios, I shall own a record company, I shall own my own hair care products, I shall own my own nail shop, I shall my own bus line in Jesus name amen.

Will your faith allow you to see what God said is already yours.

Divine Invitation for a Divine Season

I decree that I have the thoughts of God in Jesus name.
I decree that God has blessed me with a mantle to govern, regulate, and exercise authority.
This is my season to live by the wisdom that God is releasing in the earth realm.
I decree that my thoughts are about the millions God told me to ask for.
God has opened my heart to receive more.
I have received an anointing to catch up on the season I missed in Jesus name.
I receive my Solomon anointing to build the kingdom of God.
I decree this is my season of substance in Jesus name.
I decree that God has given me an anointing to ask and I shall receive.
In this season I shall dream bigger than ever.
I decree that I will unlock the supernatural of God by worship.
Thank you God for moving with the spiritual generation in Jesus name.
I decree this is my season for extravagant worship.
I declare that I have a new level of giving, I will give myself out of wealth and steward myself in wealth.
My new level of giving and worship will heal my body, mind, and spirit in Jesus name.
This is my season to walk in truth not opinion.
I decree that I will operate in truth so God can release his favor on me.
I need the favor of God to rule the nations.
I will honor my spiritual mother and father in this hour.
I decree that God moves in relationship the kingdom of God is built on relationships.
If I walk in pride God can't give me anything.
I will walk in new levels of honor in Jesus name.
I decree that in this season I will cry out for discernment there are new levels of devils.
I decree I will go after the spirit of holiness and righteousness.
I will discern between the goodness and holiness of God.
I decree that I have an understanding heart that listens to God.
I decree that I will be led by peace the potting soil of revelation.
God has given me keys and strategy in my life.
This is my season for alignment for my assignment.
I will listen to how God tells me to align my life.
I decree that God is shaping my spiritual gifts to be a powerhouse in the Lord.

I declare that my motives are pure so God can bless me for the nations.
The great "I AM" is about to show up and show out in my life in Jesus name.
I decree that I need God in every area of my life to tap into the goodness of God.
As soon as I start talking God is going to respond.
The God of Israel will not forsake me.
I decree that mercy triumphs over judgment God will not refuse me in Jesus name.
I can relate to Gods love when I'm in his presence he will not reject me.
I decree this is a season were open doors cannot be shut in Jesus name.
I declare that my cup over flows. I want the good life rivers are flowing in my life.
I decree that all demonic hindrances God is flushing out of my life all the pain of my past.
I have been pre-appointed God already walked through to make room for me there is a supernatural promotion taken place.
The trees represent a place of completion in my life.
I decree that I'm steadfast and unmovable in Jesus name.
I declare that my holiness is beautiful.
I'm a person of power and resurrection in Jesus name.
I decree that I'm flexible in this hour this is my season for creativity in Jesus name.
I am the sign and wonder, I'm assigned to my generation so God can show himself strong I decree this in Jesus name.

I'm Not Going To Hell

I decree that I'm not going to hell for wearing makeup.
For the colors of the clothes I wear or the style of clothes I wear.
I decree that I'm not going to hell for wearing jewelry in Jesus name.
I'm not going to hell for wearing wigs or hair extension.
I'm not going to hell for wearing "RED" lipstick in Jesus.
I'm not going to hell for wearing open toe shoes or high heels.
I'm not going to hell for wearing nail polish or a pedicure in Jesus name.
I decree that I can come to throne of God and pray without my head being covered. God hears my thoughts and I don't have a dolly on then in Jesus name.
I decree that as a male I'm not going to hell for not having a suit and tie on every time I go to church.

I declare that as a woman I will not go to hell for wearing pants.
I'm not going to hell for showing my shoulders in Jesus name.
I'm not going to hell because I'm attracted to the opposite sex, how else will I get a spouse.
I'm not going to hell because in my former life I got tattoos & body piercing.
I'm not going to hell because I don't dot every I and cross every T I'm only human.
I'm not going to hell because I have never been baptized or speak in tongues.

I curse every religious spirit behind this mess in Jesus name. I decree that the prophetic anointing in me will confront the demon of religion. I will no longer belong to this bondage in Jesus name God has set me free. I declare that there are no religious standards in my life in Jesus name AMEN.

The kingdom of God is not based on religion God commands us to have an apostolic lifestyle.

The Rain of God

I decree I will ask the Lord for rain in the spring time he gives showers to men.
Father let your abundant showers fall on mankind.
I ask that you pour your water on all mankind to bring a cleansing and refreshing of our spirits.
I decree that God will pour his showers on my offspring they will receive immediate deliverance in every area of their lives in Jesus name.
I decree that my offspring will say I belong to the Lord.
God will send his rain in my season so I can receive my healing, and blessings and what belongs to me.
I decree that the rain of God will stop all demonic interference in my life.
God will rise up a standard around me with his rain.
I decree there will be no more demonic flooding in my life in Jesus name.
The heavens above will rain down God's righteousness.
I decree that salvation will come forth with the rain of God.
I declare that the rain of God shall go into the crack house, bars, strip clubs, homosexual bars, the casino's, the schools, the rain will touch the prostitute on the corner, the race tracks, the rain of God will go to the corner and save the drug dealer, the rain of God will stop the bullets, and the rain shall rest upon the one trying to commit suicide at this very moment in Jesus name.

I decree that the rain of God will clean up the air wave from the filth of satan, the rain will clean up the TV shows, the rain of God will stop the demonic influence behind music in Jesus name.

I declare that the rain of God will visit each household on my block.

The rain of God will visit the lonely at heart.

I decree that the rain of God will release a sound in the spiritual realm like never before. This sound is going to go before us and fight our battles, heal our minds and give us the love of God.

The rain of God will produce fruit in my life there will be no more barren places in my life.

I decree that it will rain on the righteous and unrighteous in Jesus name.

The rain of God will release my freedom in the spirit realm.

I decree with this rain there will be such a cry for God's heart in Jesus name.

I declare that the rain of God is being released for my destiny and generations to come.

God has already measured out the water over our land.

I decree there will be an increase in every area of my life.

The blood of Jesus will continue to flow like never before.

The rain will release the hand of God in a powerful way in Jesus name.

Father God let your rain saturate me, sustain me, and keep me holy before your eyes.

God has released a plentiful rain in this season a rain of more than enough.

I decree that rain is a blessing from God.

The rain of God will dry up my tears and fears in Jesus name.

I listen for the voice of God in his rain.

God will not shut up the heavens; the heavens are open for me to receive.

I decree that my seed shall be prosperous because of the rain.

Father God drench me with your rain so I can do miracles and signs and wonders.

The rain of God shall release all bondage from my life I decree this in Jesus name.

I decree that the rain of God will move me into the vein of God.

The rain of God shall hold me and never let go.

I'm thankful that the rain of God saved me from my past people, places and things.

My soul is thirsty for the rain of God.

Only God can satisfy my thirst. In Jesus name Amen.

My Heavenly Deposit

Father God your word says I have an inheritance from you.
I decree that it is an blessing that is extend from here until we meet face to face.
It was through the last will and testament of Jesus Christ that I receive my deposit.
I thank you for the work that was done on the cross.
I pour into my heavenly deposit every time I pray God's word over the situations of my life.
I decree that present day truth makes my deposit in the heavenlies.
I declare that God predestined me to receive my inheritance from the beginning of time.
This was God preordained plan for my salvation.
I'm predestined in Christ. I receive all the promises of God.
I believe in the gospel for my salvation, I've heard the word of truth.
I'm obedient to the gospel of Christ I declare this in Jesus name.
The redemption work of Jesus is my heavenly deposit.
My faith, repentance, confession, and baptism were all a part of my heavenly deposit.
I declare that the Holy Spirit plays a big part in my inheritance.
God recognizes his holy spirit inside of us.
My heavenly inheritance will not fade away.
It is the fathers will that I receive my heavenly inheritance in Jesus name.
Transformation took place when I received my heavenly inheritance.
I decree that I'm steadfast and unmovable in my walk with Christ.
Knowing that God will never give up on me is part of my heavenly deposit.

I'm a Child of Destiny and Purpose

I decree there is greatness flowing out of me in Jesus name.
My purpose is to expand the kingdom of God through spiritual warfare.
My destiny is to bring down principalities, strongholds, and wreck the kingdom of darkness.
I decree that my purpose is to be the light to those who are still in the dark.
My destiny is my living testimony I am the walking word of God.
I was called to do greater works than Jesus.
My destiny is to walk in all authority that has been given to me.
My purpose is that demons recognize me and obey my voice.

My purpose is to be a general in the spirit in Jesus name.
My purpose is to break the strategies of satan and tear down his kingdom.
My purpose is to understand the things of God the revelation knowledge.
I have been released to be an end time warrior in Jesus name.
My purpose is to move forth to manifest the prophetic word of God.
My destiny is for God to use me as soil to produce the seed of righteousness in Jesus name.
My destiny is the soil and posture of my heart.
My purpose is to be a world changer.
My purpose is to flow with the grace of God.
My purpose is to build an apostolic background for generations to come.
I decree that there are millions of souls tied to my destiny.
My purpose is for God to get the glory out of my life I decree this in Jesus name.
My purpose is to be a mouth piece for God.
My purpose is to speak a strong word into the lives of the weak.
My purpose is to never lose my momentum and move swiftly with the hand of God.
My destiny is to tear down every religious spirit in my nation.
My destiny is to carry the apostolic word to the nations.
My purpose is to never let evil reign in my life.
My destiny is to know the thoughts, purpose, and things of God.
My purpose is to have my prophetic word find its mate.
My purpose is to close the mouths of the false prophets, tear down demonic altars, and destroy all doctrines of devils in Jesus name.
My purpose is to hold on to my corporate prophecy I declare this in Jesus name.
My purpose is the break the limitations off the mind of the weak.
My destiny is to walk in complete healing.
My destiny is to cancel the assignment of those that want to make war with the Lamb of God.
My destiny is to bring restoration back to the kingdom of God through his word.
My purpose is to fight the good fight of faith in Jesus name.
My destiny is to be a co-labor with God in the earth realm.
My destiny is not my decision but my discovery.
My purpose is to have an appetite for the things of God.
My destiny is to destroy the foundation of evil the gates of hell will not prevail against me.
My purpose is to walk in a powerful anointing from God.
My destiny is not to miss the move of God in this apostolic season in Jesus name.

He Kept Me

When death called my name Jesus wanted me more.
When I fell into sin Jesus kept me.
When the drugs were too much to bear Jesus said that enough.
When my family turned their backs on me Jesus kept me.
When suicide would not work Jesus said I have a purpose for you.
When the tears fell one after another he kept me.
When I was homeless and wanted to give up he kept me.
When depression had my mind not only did he heal me but he kept me.
The lonely nights of feeling all alone his presence let me know I was safe in his arms.
When I was lied on he kept me
When the snares and traps of the enemy thought they had me God pulled me through and kept me.
As I sat on the bar stool drinking my life away God said your destiny is in me not alcohol.
When my hands were tied behind my back God loosens the shackles and he kept me.
When rejection was my best friend God showed me what a friend I have in Jesus.
When I went through the fire he kept me.
When I had to bury the ones I love he kept me.
When that loved one died and is lost in eternity he kept me.
When my virginity was stolen away from me he kept me.
When my mind ran away from me Jesus gave me the mind of Christ and kept me.
I'm alive today because God kept me.
The rainbow in the sky is God's promise that he is keeping me.
When the spirit of python tried to squeeze the life out of me God kept me.
When the spirit of lust over took my flesh God gave me a spirit of purity and kept me.
When the spirit of oppression attacked me God freed me and kept me.
When the gates of hell came against me he kept me from falling.
I thank God that he keeps me in the palm of his hands and he will never let go!

The Voice

I decree that my voice will reach the nations.
God has given me a voice that will make the demon flee at my command.
My voice is one for the nations to break through the barriers of all principalities.
I decree I will use my voice to bless and not to curse.
I decree that with my voice I will not be afraid to say what God has spoken.
God has given me a voice with boldness in Jesus name.
I will not speak death over my life or anyone life I decree this in Jesus name.
I decree my voice is heard around the world.
Jesus will use my voice to help set the captives free.
I decree that there is great deliverance in my voice in Jesus name.
I decree I will speak that which is apostolic for the advancement of the kingdom in Jesus name.
I decree that my voice is wise and it brings wisdom for my generation and generations to come.
My voice will speak what God has laid on my heart.
I will not use my voice as a weapon against the kingdom of God.
I decree that I will speak no deception or corruption into the kingdom of God.
I decree that I will not speak judgment over my generation of generations to come.
I decree that my words are like a honeycomb sweetness to the soul and health to my body.
I declare that I will not speak any anger, wrath, malice, slander, and obscene talk with my mouth.
The Holy Spirit will use my voice to bring salvation to the generations to come.
I decree that the words of God I speak will not be void they will have life and give life.
God will justify me by the words I speak in Jesus name.
I decree that my voice is not a religious voice my voice will remove the bondage from the spirit of religion in Jesus name.
I decree that I will keep my mouth and tongue to keep me out of danger.
I decree that satan can stop my voice from reaching the nations.
Let the words of my mouth and the meditation of my heart be acceptable in your sight, O Lord, my rock and my redeemer.
I declare that I will not be hasty with my words in Jesus name.
A gentle tongue is a tree of life, but perverseness in it breaks the spirit.

I declare that I will use my voice to teach and preach the word of God.
A word fitly spoken is like apples of gold in a setting of silver.
The tongue of the wise commends knowledge, but the mouths of fools pour out folly.
The good person out of the good treasure of his heart produces good, and the evil person out of his evil treasure produces evil, for out of the abundance of the heart his mouth speaks.
Whoever restrains his words has knowledge, and he who has a cool spirit is a man of understanding.
I decree that with my voice I shall live and not die and declare the word of the Lord.
I will use my voice to speak from a spirit of discernment I will not be afraid to prophesize the truth.
For he whom God has sent utters the words of God, for he gives the Spirit without measure.
I decree that I recognize that my voice carries power and the sound of thunder in Jesus name.
I decree that I will not use my voice to bear false witness against my brother or sister in Christ.
I will not allow my voice to operate under the spirit of lying in Jesus name.
I will use my voice like God to speak things into creations, to speak things into existence; I will use my voice to silence every demonic confederacy in the name of Jesus.
For there is not a word in my tongue, but, lo, O LORD, thou knowest it altogether.

My Powerful Covenant

Father God I ask you in the name of Jesus to forgive the church for no longer honoring our covenant.
I declare that in this hour you will release a greater covenant for your kingdom builders in Jesus name.
I declare that I will walk in covenant agreement with God.
I cancel the assignment from hell to break the power of every demonic javelin that will be thrown at my covenant agreement in Jesus name.
Jesus I thank you that you operate out of covenant.
Jesus I believe that you are the fulfillment of every covenant.
I decree that if I don't walk in covenant with God I will have unnecessary problems.

I declare that I will not allow my covenant to be broken to give room for the enemy to enter my life.
My covenant keeps me in relationship with God forever I declare this in Jesus name.
I declare that I will not be a church hopper in this season.
My covenant gives me apostolic revelation of the things of God.
Father I ask that you have mercy on those who won't come into covenant with you.
Father I ask that every demonic altar that comes against your covenant will be shut down in the name of Jesus.
I declare that my obedience is based out of my covenant.
I decree that my covenant will keep me rooted and grounded in God.
I decree that my covenant carries a heavy responsibility in Jesus name.
My apostolic covenant produces stability I decree this in Jesus name.
With my covenant it is my responsibility to help restore and help someone.
I pray for those that are in spiritual blindness and don't want to be in covenant due to the sin in their lives, I command their souls to line up with the word of God and come into covenant in Jesus name.
I'm thankful for the covenant I have with my church.
I decree that being in covenant allows me to hear and follow Gods voice.
My covenant keeps me humble before God and willing to receive correction in Jesus name.
My covenant will not allow me to stay in a dark place but it will allow me to live.
Dark things will happen if I live in disobedience.
I decree that my covenant will give me discernment of dark things (evil) that's around me.
I decree that my covenant will not allow me to be around rebellious people.
I declare this is not a season for me to flip flop in God.
I decree that my covenant will not allow me to compromise in Jesus name.
My covenant has created Godly character that will produce all that God has for me.
I decree that my anointing is measured by my character in Jesus name.
My covenant anointing will get me through the door and bring an increase of favor to my life.
I cancel every demonic assignment that is assigned against my character, and anointing in Jesus name.
I declare that my covenant with God gives me a legal license to use the power of the Holy Spirit.
God has given me the right to use the power and authority that has been given to me.

My covenant gives me power over the Government, media, my region and nation in Jesus name.
I decree that I will use my covenant to pull down, throw down, build, and plant for the kingdom of God.
I decree that my covenant will get me over every mountain and obstacle in my way.
I decree that I will use my covenant to root out the deeply seeded demonic atmosphere in my region, city and nation.
My covenant will break the stronghold of religion, and traditional things that make the word of God have no effect in Jesus name.
I decree that my covenant will uproot so demons can never manifest again in Jesus name.
I declare that my covenant will break every negative word spoken against the kingdom of God I will counter act by releasing the word of God in Jesus name.
My covenant will allow me to pull down things that have been built on a demonic foundation I will pull from the heavenlies, principalities, curses, perversion, territorial spirits, and demonic strongholds in Jesus name.
The covenant that I have with God allows me to defeat the demonic realm and come forth victoriously.
I declare that my covenant breaks the satanic kingdom, and occult leaders, witches and warlocks, physics, necromancers, seers for the demonic in Jesus name.
My covenant has allowed me to build and establish God's kingdom here on earth in Jesus name.
I decree that Gods covenant shall rule and reign on earth.
I decree that my covenant will allow me to plant things that will never die spiritually in Jesus name.
I decree that my covenant will help me move strongly in the prophetic in Jesus name amen.

My Apostolic Impartation

I decree that I will use my apostolic impartation to cause activation for the kingdom of God.
My apostolic impartation allows me to be a mover and a shaker of demonic forces that have been in the way centuries.
I decree that I will not stay stuck in a place that I'm familiar with in Jesus name.

I declare that people around me will be able to shift things in the spiritual realm.
I decree that the days of normal church is over in Jesus name.
I have ears that hear and receive from the spiritual realm.
I will not allow my personality to change the word God has spoken over my life in Jesus name.
I decree that God has given me the power to impart teaching, preaching, and lying on of hands.
God's impartation has given me a jump in my spirit.
I declare that God has released a supply of his anointing for impartation.
I decree that I will not get filled to get empty.
I will go into the land were no man has gone before and preach and teach with my apostolic impartation.
I declare that the demons of hell no my voice and must obey me in Jesus name.
My apostolic impartation will break the doctrines of devils I declare this in Jesus name.
I declare that my apostolic impartation will open up the mysteries of the gospel to me.
My anointing will not allow me to be deceived in Jesus name.
I claim what is rightfully mine and use my weapon as an end time warrior for God.
I declare that my apostolic anointing releases me from any demonic bondage.
I will stay up under the covering of God in Jesus name.
I will not escalate my gift higher than my anointing in Jesus name.
My apostolic impartation will break through atmosphere controlled by evil so the spirit of God can enter in.
In this season I will not reason with the word of God.
I declare that my apostolic anointing will remove every spirit that opposes the move of God.
I declare that my anointing will cause my enemy to bow down before me in Jesus name.
I decree that I will use my present day anointing to upgrade the people and movement of God.
I declare that I will never speak from a defeated state in Jesus name.
I declare I will line up my mouth with the move of God.
I will not use my anointing to go against the spirit of God.
My apostolic anointing gave me an apostolic upgrade in Jesus name.
I decree that only those that hear from God will receive an apostolic anointing.
I will use my apostolic anointing to control the nations for the kingdom of God in Jesus name.
I have taken on a new level of praise with my apostolic anointing.

My Apostolic Culture

I declare that I walk in authority and boldness in Jesus name.
I declare that I display my culture and values of my apostolic culture.
I declare that my foundation with Jesus is my doctrine.
When I walk in my apostolic culture I cannot be defeated in Jesus name.
I decree that I have authority over anything that comes against me from hell.
I decree that the enemy can't tap into my mental realm in Jesus name.
My apostolic culture will not let me walk in defeat but in authority.
I declare that God gave me specific instruction for my culture.
I decree that my apostolic culture cannot be uprooted by demons or man.
I am the seal of apostleship in Jesus name.
I belong to an apostolic house.
I walk with my shield of faith in Jesus name.
I am a spiritual sign of readiness I'm qualified for the apostolic.
God has prepared me for my apostolic culture.
God has established me as genuine and true.
I decree that my seal from God gives me comfort and understanding in Jesus name.
I declare that only God can judge my eternal state man can only see my fruits.
I declare that every time I open my mouth to pray I stop all demonic assignments with my seal of apostleship in Jesus name.
I declare that my seal is my tattoo in the spirit realm what God called me to be.
God sealed me so the world will know that I have been sent in Jesus name.
I have an inward seal that can't be erased I declare this in Jesus name.
My seal is the backbone of the core of my apostolic culture.

Refresh Me

Refresh my soul blow your breath upon me.
Were my heart has been broken heal it with the blood of Jesus.
Mend all the breaks and tears inside of me refresh me O'Lord I pray.
Refresh me with a double portion of your anointing.
Restore to me the days of my youth.
I decree that a refreshing of your waters will flow over my life.
Refresh my spirit were it is weak.
Refresh me with a new rest from God.
Refresh my heart so I can love again.
Refresh every drought in me in Jesus name.

Refresh the gospel that is inside of me.
Stir up your gifts inside of me so that I may be able to use them.
Refresh me with boldness.
Refresh the winds that blow over my life.
Refresh me with your joy and happiness.
Refresh me with your presence in Jesus name.
Refresh the apostolic inside of me.
Refresh the prophetic inside of me.
Refresh the hurt and pain that you will remove and replace it with you love and understanding.
Refresh me with your rest that I may give you all my burdens.
Refresh me I can be sensitive and follow the leading of the Holy Spirit.
As I rest in you God restore my soul.
Thank you for your wonderful promise to refresh us in Jesus name.
Refresh me when I get weary.
I accept your refreshing and restoration in Jesus name.
Father God give me wisdom so I know when to slow down.
Lead me beside the still waters so I can be refreshed.
As you refresh me I will distribute your living waters to help desperate for you.
I decree I will allow my soul to be restored.
God I ask that you refresh and restore my offspring in Jesus name.
Refresh my soul to come alive.
Refresh my memory of what you have done for me and how far you have brought me.
As you awaken me to Christ let your will be done.
Refresh you as you enlarge me in Jesus name.
Let the flood from heaven refresh my soul.
The word of God encourages me to ask for a daily refreshing in Jesus name amen.

The Fire of God

Father God I ask you to release your fire to burn out all the disobedience in the body of Christ.
Let the fire of God expose all the hidden agenda in the pull pits in Jesus name.
I decree that the fire of God will burn the truth into the body of Christ.
Let the fire of God expose every hidden homosexual and lesbian spirit in the body of Christ.

I decree that the fire of God will make me live a life of holiness in Jesus name.
I decree that the fire of God will expose all my hidden sin in Jesus name.
I decree that the fire of God will keep me in obedience in Jesus name.
The fire of God will make you have violent faith to take your city, region, and nation I decree this in Jesus name.
I thank you God that the Holy Spirit appears by the fire of God.
Let the fire of God burn up every witch and warlocks prayers and plans against the body of Christ.
By your fire God visit every witch and warlock and save their souls.
I decree that the fire of God will bring the sinner to repentance in Jesus name.
My spirit is on fire for the things of God.
The word of God is like fire in my bones.
I decree that the fire of God will lead me to the one closest to hell in Jesus name.
Let the fire fall for us as it did in Elijah's day.
The fire of God will burn up the cancer, HIV, hypertension, mental illness, diabetes; heart attacks, strokes, I decree that my body must line up with the word of God.
Whether it is the refiner fire or the fire of God let it be released on all flesh and blood in Jesus name.
Let the fire of God pass judgment on every demonic altar, false prophets, false apostles, false minister, and silence them in Jesus name.
I decree that the fire of God will build Godly character in me.
I decree that the fire of God will make the crooked paths straight before me.
I decree that our God is a consuming fire.
The fire of God will make you hunger and thirst for the word of God.
I decree that the fire of God will make you humble in his presence.
I decree that the fire of God will rebuild me from the inside and out.
I will allow the fresh fire of God to burn within me to release the living water inside of me.
I decree that I will stay on fire for God so the enemy will have no room in my life.
My tongue is on fire for God I decree this in Jesus name.
The fire and power of God moves in my ministry,
I decree that the living fire that is inside of me will boil when God adds his fire to it.
I decree that the fire of God will burn all the briers and thorns in my life.
With the fire of God over my life the demons will flee from me.
I decree that the fire of God will make the devil bring back everything he stole from me one-hundred fold in Jesus name amen.

Everything that God created will see the fire of God I decree this in Jesus name.
The fire of God will burn up all the wicked in the earth.
I decree that my life is purified with the fire of God.
I decree that the fire of God will stop all death and premature death from attacking me in Jesus name.
I decree that the fire of God is a covering for me in Jesus name.
I decree that the fire of God has kept me holy and set apart.
I declare that the world cannot put out the fire of God inside of me.
I decree that the fire of God is my purification, and cleansing in Jesus name.
I decree that the fire of God is the hedge of protection that surrounds me.

I Will Immerse In the Glory

I decree that the Glory of God can been seen in my life in Jesus name.
I declare that I am sent by God with a purpose.
I thank God that he does not condemn me for having a past there was no glory in that story.
I decree that I will keep my eye on the prize and win souls for the kingdom of God.
I'm called to shift the atmosphere for God.
I decree that nothing from my past can harm my future.
I declare that I'm not a failure to God he gave me his spirit to carry.
Were God brought me from has no power to keep me from Gods glory.
I decree that the world will see the glory of God.
I decree that I live in my future in Jesus name.
I decree that I learned how to take conviction and turn it into repentance in Jesus name.
My apostolic seal is what God uses to deputize me.
I decree that the glory of God glows from the inside to the outside of me.
God will take me from glory to glory in Jesus name.
I declare that the glory of God gives me provision, protection, and promotion in Jesus name.
I do not belong to a powerless church my church is a kingdom builder in my church you will see signs and wonders and miracles performed I decree this in Jesus name.
I'm not arrogant that is the glory of God inside of me.
I decree it is time to operate from what God has put inside of me.
The devil can't stand the glory of God over my life.

I decree that I am the image of Christ on earth.
I declare that you can't curse what God has blessed in my life.
I declare that living a saved lifestyle is not bondage in Jesus name.
The glory of God has set me free from legalism and a religious spirit in Jesus name.
I declare that true holiness is to please God.
The glory of God is the center to the piece in my life.

Spiritual Waters over Me

I thank you that the waters in my life represent the Holy Spirit.
I curse the water levels that come to my ankles I command every spirit of confusion to leave in Jesus name.
I decree that when the waters level reach my knees it will bring humility to my spirit.
I declare that I rely on the Holy Spirit for advancement in the kingdom of God.
The waters of God will give me a fresh prayer life in Jesus name.
The waters over my life make me reverence the spirit of God.
I decree that the waters over me gives me a new beginning a new awakening in the spirit.
I declare a spiritual manifestation in my life in Jesus name.
The spiritual waters over my life give me victory I every area in Jesus name.
I decree that the waters over my life give me a deeper connection with my heavenly father.
I declare that my mind is at peace in Jesus name.
The spiritual waters of God pulled me from a place that I never want to go back to in Jesus name.
I declare that the water that runs over my life is my spiritual hedge of protection.
I decree that the spiritual waters that run over me released me from my Egypt in Jesus name.
The waters of God remind me that I have a victorious future in Christ.
The levels of water over my life will bring me into my greatness my promises from God.
I decree that there has been a spiritual pronouncement regarding my life in Jesus name.
I decree that I received my heritage from the water levels in my life.
I decree that the water levels in my life will keep me postured in Jesus name.

I decree that my water level will have to rise so I can function in my fullness.
I decree that my water level will keep me from eating at everybody table and keep me from dirty waters there will be no demonic parasites attached to me in Jesus name.
I thank God that his spiritual water will remove everything in my life that is not of God.
I decree that the water levels over my life will keep me from turning back to sin in Jesus name.
The river of God floods over me in Jesus name.
I declare that I will not drift away or fall from my spiritual covering.
This is the kind of river that I just cannot pass over in Jesus name.
I declare that I must maintain a constant water level in Jesus name.
I'm flowing in the same direction as the water levels over my life in Jesus name.
I declare that in the waters of God the devil can't locate me in Jesus name.
The water level over my life will cause a supernatural harvest for me and my offspring I declare this in Jesus name.
I decree there is a purpose for the water levels in my life.
The higher the levels of water is the higher level of spiritual warfare that I can do I decree this in Jesus name.
The spiritual water of God will heal the secrets hurts and deal with the dirty issues in my life.
The spiritual water of God will remove the dry dessert places, and the baron places in my life I decree this in Jesus name.
My water level will stop the devil from attacking what I'm doing for the kingdom of God.
Out of my heart flows rivers of "Living Water" I declare this in Jesus name.
I decree that I will never be thirsty again in Jesus name.
I decree that with the water levels over my life I have defeated the kingdom of darkness in Jesus name amen.

Canceling the Attacks from Hell

I expose every hidden trap and snare of the devil from my life, my offspring, and the body of Christ.
I decree that I'm strong in the Lord and I've overcome every attack against my life in Jesus name.
I close the mouth of every demon speaking against me in the name of Jesus.

I decree that every time written curse released against me is cancelled in Jesus name.
The attacks from hell tell me that I'm on the right path.
The blood of Jesus covers and protects me in Jesus name.
I declare that the weapon may form but it will not prosper.
I will not give the enemy any authority over that which concerns me in Jesus name.
I heard the word of the Lord and I received it in Jesus name.
I'm a pioneer a mover for the kingdom God that is why people misunderstand me and mistreat me in Jesus name.
I decree that I will confront the devil and cast him out in Jesus name.
I decree that every demonic seed that was planted in my life is uprooted in Jesus name.
I will walk steady and stable for God.
The gates of hell will not prevent me from the move of God in my life.
I will not hold on to any demon in my life and use the excuse that God is still working on me in Jesus name.
I will not die before my time no matter what demons come my way I decree this in Jesus name.
I decree that the enemy will not attack the corporate prophesy spoken in Jesus name.
The warfare is broken over the prophetic word in my life I decree this in Jesus name.
The devil cannot out do the works of God.
I decree that no devil in hell will make me lose my momentum.
Father God I ask that you reveal every human devil in my pathway in Jesus name.
The kingdom of darkness will not destroy my seed in Jesus name.
I will not except any form of harassment from the devil.
Satan I declare that I tie your hands behind your back in Jesus name.
Every day I fight for my life the enemy can never destroy me or my offspring.
I cancel the assignment of demonic wisdom off of my life in Jesus name.
I decree that no doctrines of devil will enter into my spirit.
I declare that victory belongs to the strong in faith.
I decree that I will not believe the lies of the enemy.
I cancel satan's assignment against the bible, the word of God, and my prayer life in Jesus name.
I tear down every stronghold and attack from satan over my life in the name of Jesus.
I bind every power cursing my destiny into effectiveness, in the name of Jesus.

I smash every plan of satan formed against me this year in the name of Jesus.
I turn the evil devices of witchcraft upside down in the name of Jesus.
I cancel the assignment of every ungodly and satanic thoughts I receive the mind of Christ in Jesus name.
I take authority over all demons of the night, bad dreams, nightmares, and sex dreams, and anything trying to get into my dreams. I command you to stay away in Jesus name.
In Jesus name I pull out all fiery darts, spears, voodoo, all witchcraft and curses and return it to the pits of hell in Jesus name.
I declare that my eyes are open to every trick, plan and snare of the devil in Jesus name.

Wait on the Timing of God

Father God I thank you that your timing and plans for my life are always right on time.
I call forth every person God called to bless me to come forth in God's timing in the name of Jesus.
I decree that every blessing that God has sent my way and I missed to come back around to me.
I declare that in Gods timing I will be able to bless the saved and unsaved.
I ask for patience and not rely on my flesh father I ask that you keep me from messing up your timing.
In Gods timing the window of heaven will be open over my life.
The nations are my inheritance and I claim what is mine in Jesus name.
I trust in God with all my heart and his promises will come to pass over my life.
I decree that I need the power of God to work in my life in Jesus name.
I declare that I will not miss the move of God in this season.
God is putting me on the minds of my enemies to be a blessing to me in Jesus name.
I will not give up or give in I'm determined to wait on the Lord.
I declare that God has a different perspective and sees the entire picture of my life.
God's divine order will be done in his perfect timing.
I declare that God will work his timing in my life through my prayers in Jesus name.
While I'm waiting on the hand of God to move I will believe in my prayers.
I renounce every spirit of unbelief in Jesus name I believe.

I declare that my prayers and voice is effective and powerful.
I will remain in God and he will remain in me.
I will have peace in my life while I wait on the move of God I declare this in Jesus name.
I believe that in God's perfect timing it shall come to pass.
I cancel the assignment of every demonic force that tries to stop the timing of God in Jesus name.
I'm resting in God and believing in him for everything that concerns me.
I renounce any spirits of anger, and depression as I wait patiently on God.
I will stay in an attitude of faith.
When God starts something in my life he will finish it in the name of Jesus.
God will bring my dreams to pass and answer my prayers. The answer will come, and it will be right on time in Jesus name.
The timing of God was perfect when he changed me, saved me and rearranged me.

Apostolically Walking Stable

I command everyone that God has appointed to bless me to come forth in Jesus name.
I decree that I will keep my heart with all diligence.
In my stable walk I decree that God has given me the ability to be a blessing to the kingdom.
I curse every false apostle that has ever spoken into me, prayed for me; I break the curse of slavery, greed, self-promotion in Jesus name.
I decree that I will bear the fruit of the spirit no false fruit will be produced in my life in Jesus name.
I declare that I have a planting anointing for the kingdom of God in Jesus name.
I feel the stirring on the inside of me the spirit of Nibeh has been released on me in Jesus name; I can speak from a spirit of inspiration.
I thank God that he will drop his word from heaven to help me walk stable in Jesus name.
The heavens have opened up over my life I declare this in Jesus name.
Father God I ask that you release your milk and wine over my life to bring prosperity, and abundance.
I decree that the kingdom of God is inside of me.
I declare that when the spiritual man shows up the carnal man must vacate in Jesus name.
I decree that the prophetic will change me and my offspring.

I command all churches to take there post and prepare for the move of God. My church will be an altar for the visitation of God I declare this in Jesus name.

Father God I ask that you open the eyes of every believer that they can be converted to be a Christian but not converted to the kingdom. I desire the kingdom of God.

My prophetic worship will keep me stable in the name of Jesus.

I declare that my anointing will cause demons to show up and deliverance to take place in Jesus name.

God I ask that you take my spirit to the places that my human mind can't go. Let my anointing keep me stable and take me to new levels in Jesus name.

My voice will speak and help the saints of God understand that the move of God is not of the devil. I pray they will receive a fresh revelation of the apostolic in Jesus name.

God I ask that you expose every human devil in my path that is assigned to bring fear, failures, into my life, expose every demonic gatekeeper that is assigned to keep me in bondage in Jesus name.

I cancel the assignment from demons assigned to my mind to keep me from receiving the revelation and word of God.

I curse the voices from telling me I'm not stable in God in Jesus name.

My challenges in my life keep me stable in Jesus name.

I decree that the pioneer inside of me is what satan is afraid of.

I will measure my season and walk the straight and narrow.

I declare that I can't have a dirty heart filled with dirty soil and walk stable in Jesus name.

Father God I ask that you help me face all my obstacles what I don't deal with today will knock on my door tomorrow.

God I ask that you divinely subtract from my life the things not of you.

I will keep my momentum to walk stable in Jesus name.

Apostle Heart

Father God I ask you in Jesus name that you let me govern with my apostolic heart.

I free myself from the initial excitement then not following through with the things of God.

I declare that the body of Christ will move in momentum corporately in Jesus name.

After I have gone through all my trials I declare that I will still be excited in Christ.

I decree that I will guard the stature of my spirit in Jesus name.
With my apostolic heart I will walk in wisdom and understanding.
I'm in a local place with a global expectation from Christ.
I will not reject the knowledge that God is trying to give me in Jesus name.
I decree that as the Holy Spirit guides me I will give impartation, preach, teach, anoint, and lay hands upon the children of God.
I declare that I am filled with an animated quickening.
I decree that I am a risk taker, free from criticism, and mission minded in Jesus name.
God gave me a heart to understand and learn and to advance his kingdom.
I declare that God has taken me places in the spirit where no man has ever been before in Jesus name.
I decree that my destiny is not my decision it is my discovery in Christ.
I came into the earth realm to discover what I am to do for God I declare this in Jesus name.
My heart has an appetite for the apostolic and kingdom mined things of God.
Thank you God for given me your grace to get into the kingdom in Jesus name.
I declare that I must serve to be sent.
I must know how to build and battle at the same time in Jesus name.
I declare that I am serving my way to greatness in Jesus name.
I understand what God is doing in a corporate setting in Jesus name.
God don't have a lie in his mouth.
I will help God by being a co-labor in the earthly realm in Jesus name.
With an apostolic heart I cannot hold on to the sin from my past. I'm delivered from my past fears and tears I decree this in Jesus name.
I can't quit now God has not given me a spirit to give up.
In the heat of the battle I know that God did not change his mind about the plans for my life God is not an indian giver in Jesus name.
I decree that my heart and mind thinks like God.
God I ask that you help me to be pure while I do your will.
The prayers that I pray are birthing out of my heart to do the will of God.
I'm walking in my breakthrough in Jesus name.
I declare my victory in Jesus name no devil in hell can stop my anointing from reaching the kingdom for God.
I will be obedient to what called me to do in the earthly realm.
The blood of Jesus is powerful enough to pull me from my past hurts, mistakes.
I don't worry about what people say about me my pass helps me understand who I am in Christ.
I decree that I will surrender all of me to Jesus and let him take control and use me as an end time warrior for the movement in the kingdom.

My Spiritual Mate

I decree that no man or women can anoint themselves in Jesus name.
I must have a pure heart to go before Jesus.
I declare that sweet aroma of my spirit will lead people to Christ.
When my spiritual mate comes it will not be a hindrance but it will be advancement in the kingdom.
What is not helping me is hurting me and I have no time to get left behind.
My spiritual mate will not hinder my progress I will spiritually grow.
I declare that I will not die before my time no matter what demon comes my way.
God is opening opportunities for me the doors are open for me and no one but God can shut them.
I will never put my mouth on the work that God is doing.
I decree that everything God has said has a mate in Jesus name.
Demons have no spiritual hold on me I declare this is Jesus name.
I curse the devil from trying to block the corporate prophesy over me.
God has freed me so I won't go back to bondage.
My spiritual mate is one with God.
I decree that every prophetic word I have spoken has life to it my word shall live and not die.
I'm walking with a positive spirit there is nothing negative in me in Jesus name.
I'm expecting my spirit to catch up with the word spoken over me.
I decree that me and my spirit man must line up with the word of God I command this in Jesus name.
Father God I ask that you do a deep cleansing of my mind body and soul.
My spirit man jumps every morning when I wake up this is the day my prophecy shall come to pass.
I decree that I'm breeding grounds for miracles in Jesus name.
I have broken the limitation off me spiritually my spirit is at a state of expectation.
I'm to mature in Christ to go backward.
My spiritual mate pulls me forward to the things of God.
If God can part the red sea he can part the reds sea in your life.
God will speak over the secret places in my heart and shield every attack directed at my heart.
My word is in the atmosphere looking for its mate, I will keep my guard up for the counterfeit word that will try to enter my atmosphere.
I will allow God to be God in my life.
I need the thoughts, plans and purpose of God for my life.
I'm expecting my prophetic word to find its mate.
God word is for sure, I won't run after the false prophetic word

Apostolic Momentum

I will advance the kingdom through the rule and reign of Christ.

I decree that God will never allow the devil to outdo him.

Father God I thank you that you allow the attacks of the enemy so you can supernaturally show up.

God I ask that you expose anything trying to kill my momentum in Jesus name.

I declare that I will not limit my miracles to a physical move all my miracles will be creative.

My faith has perimeters called wisdom in Jesus name.

God has shown me in dreams all the plans and tricks of the enemy against my family, marriage, children and fiancés in Jesus name.

My second wind is about to be stirred up by God.

I decree that I will not let no religious spirit kill my momentum every movement in me is fresh and new.

God is getting ready to come after me to put me on a wave to give me more momentum and miracles I declare this in Jesus name.

I'm covered with a label from God that says I'm victorious and more than a conqueror.

I understand the protective elements of the prophetic word spoken over me in Jesus name.

I declare that I value and will grab ahold of what God has said over me.

The people that surround me are interested in the things of God.

Thank you God for being acquainted with my feelings in Jesus name.

I will stay fresh and sensitive to the word of God.

I declare that staying fresh will confuse the adversary in Jesus name.

I will not let anyone talk me out of my dreams.

I decree that I'm excited about the things of God.

I will value the word from God before I value the word of man.

I will guard my ear gates from demonic seeds that will try to produce a harvest in my life.

Everyone does not understand my anointing that is why they are wolves in sheep clothing.

I will never let what the devil has said about me be true I decree this in Jesus name.

I cancel every demonic fly that is attracted to my anointing I release the blood of Jesus against them.

I declare that after my next victory there is going to be an enemy against me and I cancel the assignment of the enemy right now in Jesus name.

I will stay under my covering in Jesus name so the enemy will not have any room to attack me.
I cancel the assignment of every demonic javelin thrown at me I break this word curse and say that you are void of life and have no meaning in Jesus name.
I decree that as long as I stay under to anointing of God every demonic javelin will slip by me.
Every demonic messenger that is assigned to guide me off track I curse your assignment I decree that I will complete the apostolic kingdom work God has for me.
I will not fall back to what God has delivered me from in Jesus name.
God has already sent his strong word to move me out of complacency and stagnation.
I decree that I can't do kingdom work in my own strength in Jesus name.
The voice of God is my declaring factor I hear and I obey.
I decree that God has given me his grace to move in momentum.
My goal is to get souls saved and be the light in the dark I decree this in Jesus name.
The prophetic came to challenge the voices of complacency to bring correction in the church, get me delivered from religion, and to raise the dead and cast out devils in Jesus name.
God desire is to have prophetic people his grace sets me apart.
I decree that I will not rely on my flesh to build the kingdom.
God has given me the vision and he will supply the resources in Jesus name.
I repent of anything I tried to do in my own flesh to build God's kingdom.
From this day forward I will rely on God's strength to accomplish his will on earth.
The enemy can't handle my upgrade in advancing the kingdom.

Recognize, Raise, Reform and Release

Father God I ask that you raise me up to release your prophetic word in Jesus name.
Raise up your people so the body of Christ can be rebuilt and honored once again.
Expose every false and demonic pulpit in Jesus name.
I decree that there will be teams to impact the nation the time has come to come forth and declare the name of the Lord.

I release an anointing of responsibility to activate and move in the kingdom of God.
I decree there will be a fresh movement like never before in Jesus name.
There will be a new refreshing to reform the body of Christ.
Father I ask that all dead weight be moved out of the way search our hearts and mind so we can restructure your kingdom in Jesus name.
We will relaunch with a greater strength we a force not to be reckon with.
The fire of God will burn with in us to take true revival to the nations and bring about true repentance in Jesus name.
I'm an apostolic person and I thrive in diversity I will not become quite in the storm.
I declare that my heart is open to God and this is the greatest time for reformation in Jesus name.
In the midst of my persecution I still will stand strong I will not back down or give up.
I decree that I will not get stuck in religious church mentality in Jesus name.
I declare that I will operate in deliverance and a revivalist anointing.
I am a revivalist and I will face some persecution.
The grip of the religious spirit will be removed from the body of Christ I declare this in Jesus name.
My persecution will keep me on track it will show the real me.
My persecution is pushing me out for the advancement of the kingdom.
As an apostolic reformer and revivalist the religious system is afraid of me.
God labels me as a world changer.
I decree that I am moving forth to manifest the prophetic word.
God has given me good soil to produce the seed that he requires in my life.
My posture and heart is right so my seed will manifest in Jesus name.
I will not allow calcium to build up on the word that is inside of me.
God will always honor my movement.
I decree that my heart is in a place of endurance.
I will protect my seed and vision in Jesus name.
When I reform the nations I will bring back the mentality of the doctrine of God in Jesus name.
Everyone will not believe the word of God so father I ask that you prepare their hearts and minds to receive in Jesus name.
I thank that the truth in your word will reach the minds of the lost.
I decree that the spirits of the unsaved will be open to receive in Jesus name.
With this reformation we will bring change, renovation, and make corrections, bring truth into regions that have never heard the word of God.

As a reformer I have to walk in a spirit of boldness and be faithful to my calling in Jesus name.
I declare that my testimony of truth will bring the people out.
I call forth every apostolic reformer to take their post in Jesus name.
I decree there is a call to the nations.
I do not look like or act like the religious system in Jesus name.
I cancel every spirit of intellectualism, and every spirit that tries to twist the word of God.
I declare that as an apostolic reformer I stand for apostolic doctrine in Jesus name.
I decree that I have heart knowledge I live it and walk it out.
I hear the truth in the spirit.

What Happens When I don't Study

Forgive me father for making my day stressful by not studying your word.
When I don't studying I'm telling God that I don't love him.
I decree that I will not study just to debate with people the word of God will speak for itself.
I won't be under a demonic assignment to study the word and argue it.
We should not mix the law (Old Testament) with grace (New Testament).
I decree we live off the grace of God.
I decree that I won't read my bible to make myself look good.
When I don't study I make my spiritual man weak I repent from not studying to show myself approved.
I will not talk foolishly about the bible.
Father I ask that you give me revelation and knowledge of your word so I can take it to the nations.

Exercising Your Authority

There is power behind the word of God that I speak I decree this in Jesus name.
My fruits will show how I exercise my authority.
I decree that there is always a battle that I am fighting that is why I exercise my God given authority.
I declare that even when I'm weak I have authority in Jesus name.
By me being holy and righteous I can use the name of Jesus.

I will never use the name of God in vain I decree this in Jesus name.
I daily exercise my authority in Jesus name.
Every demonic assignment knows the power and authority and weight that the word of God carries that is why I use it in authority.
I decree that I exercise my authority through the blood of Jesus.
I know that I am a overcomer everything that was designed to kill me made me stronger in God.
Thank you satan for all the tricks, schemes, and plans against my life it made me the prayer warrior that I am today I decree this in Jesus name.
I refuse to be tossed to and fro I'm a warrior I stand strong.
I declare that I use praise and worship as a way to exercise my authority in Jesus name.
I pierce my way through demonic dimension in Jesus name.
My first priority is the kingdom of God.
I decree that the apostolic is the driving force inside of me.
Jesus is the Lord over the church he is the reflection of his father.
I declare that my apostolic spirit has me on fire for the kingdom of God.
My prophecy is the element of warfare I declare this is Jesus name.
With my prophecy and authority I push back all demonic forces in Jesus name.
I decree that the mantle that I wear provokes devils and demons my mantle had to get bloody.
My authority fights for the word spoken over my life in Jesus name.
The word of God works no matter where I am at I declare this in Jesus name.
I decree that hell is having a nervous breakdown due to my authority.
I declare that I function in being the sent one in Jesus name.
My authority has called me to understand governmental things if the government is out of order the church can't function in Jesus name amen.

Demonic Flies

Father God in Jesus name I expose every demonic fly that has tried to nest, breed or hatch in my life.
I curse you flies and cancel every demonic effect and side effect in Jesus name.
I command that you can never lay or leave eggs on my spirit the blood of Jesus is against you.
I cancel every spiritual attraction from the flies off of my mind, body, spirit, ministry, fiancés, and my creativity in Jesus name.

I cancel the sting of every demonic bee that was attracted to my lifestyle in Jesus name.
Every curse that came along with the flies I cancel it in Jesus name.
I decree that I no longer have a demonic aroma attached to my life but the sweet fragrance from the Holy Spirit.
I declare that my body is healed all sickness that came from demonic flies no longer can live in my body in Jesus name.
I command the spirit of Beelzebub to come out from hiding and I order you to the pits of hell you are no king or ruler or lord in my life in Jesus name.
I break the grips of Beelzebub off the body of Christ let every curse be turned around to destroy the kingdom of darkness in Jesus name.
Father God I ask that you expose all hidden and secret flies in my life in Jesus name.
I bind and rebuke every cockatrice that has come against me in Jesus name.
I bind and cast out all demonic flies that have tried to attach themselves to my anointing in Jesus name.
I loose myself from all garbage that comes from others, myself, and leaders that would attract flies into my life in Jesus name.
I declare that every demon is expose that works covertly in my life and in the life of my offspring in Jesus name.
I repent from any unconfessed sin that is attracting demonic flies in my life purge me and purify me God make me holy in Jesus name.
I put all my sin under the blood of Jesus.
I declare that I will have nothing to do with gossip, anger, bitterness, unforgiveness, pride, unbelief, self-promotion for these spirits carry demonic flies in Jesus name.

Demonic Crabs

I cancel the assignment of all demonic crabs that always tries to keep my life in a pinch or in stressful situations in Jesus name.
I declare that I will not walk in a spirit of feeling overwhelmed and stressed out in Jesus name.
I will keep walking in the fruit of the spirit and not in defeat I decree this in Jesus name.
I cancel every spirit of rage and anger associated with all demonic crabs.
I declare that no demonic crab will grab hold nor steal my anointing in Jesus name.
I will flow in my apostolic, kingdom minded anointing, I walk in the love of Jesus.

I decree that I will not ever allow a demonic crab to take root in my life and God while you are at it remove all the crabby humans out of my life in Jesus name.

I will not allow any demonic crab to keep me in spiritual blindness Father God I ask that you expose and deliver me from all demonic crabs in Jesus name I pray amen.

Demonic Eyeballs

I blind every demonic eyeball that has followed my life, or lead me down the wrong pathway in Jesus name.

I decree that no demonic eye will have insight into my soul.

I declare that no demonic eyeball will not stop the prophecy from coming to past in my life the vision that God has given me will be carried out in Jesus name.

Every demonic eye that tries to stay close to my spirit the blood of Jesus has already conquered it.

No demonic eye will cause me to walk with a zigzag spirit of never knowing where I'm headed to in Jesus name. I will walk in the path that Jesus has cleared for me.

I will keep my spiritual eyes on what God has for me no longer will I look to my left or to my right.

I decree that I'm no longer directionless I have a plan and a purpose for the kingdom of God in Jesus name amen.

Power of Being Unified

I decree that I have been in training for the raining in Jesus name.

Every storm in my life has had a purpose.

I decree that from this day forward God is doing away with personality driven churches.

I'd rather be a amateur in the new that a professional in the old way of doing things.

I declare that worship will soften a heart of stone in Jesus name.

Father God I ask that you keep my church unified so we can affect the nations.

I decree that all churches will embrace what God is doing in this season.

I expect persecution as long as I am a pioneer for God.

I declare that I will stay pure with in my spirit in Jesus name.
I will put my flesh behind me and pray for those that purposely do me wrong in Jesus name.
I repent for wiping my prayers out of the heavenlies by speaking against the word of God.
I declare that I will dwell in the land of good speaking in Jesus name.
As long as there is unity in my church God will come down to see what we are doing
Father God please help me to keep my heart pure and help my church family keep their heart pure so we will be in unity so the Glory of God will shine upon us.
I decree that the enemy cannot stop a unified army.
I cancel the assignment of jealousy, division, strife, gossip and envy from entering our church service in Jesus name.
In this season I will not be able to speak from an eight track mindset in an IPod generation.
I will speak the truth and I cancel the assignment of deception that comes to steal the truth from Gods people in Jesus name.
I decree that I will doctrine myself with words that will bring liberty.
My church is a trend setter for the apostolic to birth in my region in Jesus name.
I and my father are one it take relationships to have oneness in the kingdom of God.
I declare that I will keep my promise to spread the gospel to all nations in Jesus name.
My reflection will reproduce where I come from that is my obedience and commitment.
I declare that truth revealed is the level of warfare I'm in.
The stronger my gift the stronger my grace is in Jesus name.
I decree that the apostolic did not die when Peter died I am living proof of apostolic for this generation.
I call forth all fellow labors of Christ to arise and get in proper position for the kingdom of God.
We are called to be the model church that will bring in souls by the millions.
The truth is being pioneered out of our mouths I cancel the assignment of criticism in the name of Jesus.
I declare that I'm in training for the raining I will endure hardness as a good solider in Jesus name.
We are birthing a new pattern in this season we are the frontrunners for Jesus.
I declare that the enemy is not done attacking us we are in our greatest hour.

I decree that we are making the climate conducive for the spirit of God to take over in Jesus name.
The church is getting out of bondage and coming into the newness of Christ.
I decree that we have predominating influence to exercise the governing of God.
I have to be willing to follow the cloud and not the crowds I will not be a people pleaser in this season.
In this season I'm governing my atmosphere I declare this in Jesus name.

Momentum

I declare that the fire of God burns on the inside of me this is what helps keeps my momentum stable.
In this season God is doing a great work inside of me in Jesus name.
My momentum is fighting the demons that try to stop churches from growing.
The words that proceed out of my mouth let them be truth in Jesus name.
I decree that I walk in servant hood.
The glory of God wants to send me into dark places to bring deliverance and activate the Holy Spirit I declare this in Jesus name.
I decree that in this season God is raising up generals to do his deliverance and I will be one of the generals.
I will keep a fresh anointing to walk with momentum.
I will reach people with the present day truth of God's word I declare this in Jesus name.
My momentum has taken me from the gutter most to the utter most.
I decree that I have reached a place in the realm of the spirit that there is no turning back.
I'm being attacked but I still keep growing and moving forth.
I will not allow a spirit of offense to nest in my spirit I decree this in Jesus name.
The pressure of life and this world will not stop my momentum from going forth.
My momentum moves at Gods speed.
My momentum is the likeness of God on earth.
I will reach the people who never knew about momentum in Jesus name.
I refuse to backslide in my momentum I have God given passion, and zeal.
God will release his momentum for the things that need to be done for the kingdom in Jesus name.
I decree that my lifestyle brings momentum to life.

My momentum has moved me away from my old ways in Jesus name.
I declare that momentum will allow me to go through the trials that I go through in Jesus name.
I decree that momentum will not slow me down in Jesus name.
I declare that my momentum will cause the next generation to be happy to do God's work.

My Past Does Not Matter

I decree that this is the year that I will rule in the midst of my enemies.
I thought I was living until I had an encounter with Jesus.
When I thought I was in a strong place God showed me my weakness.
I declare that my weakness from my past is what made me strong.
God used my mess when I was in my mess to not only pull me out but to get my undivided attention in Jesus name.
I don't care what the religious system says about my past it's all about the kingdom work God has for me.
I'm thankful for the grace of God every time I said I was not going to do it I found myself doing it again.
I decree that I will not sit in church and pretend that I don't have issues in Jesus name.
I declare that the power of my past has no control over me in my present day.
There are souls waiting on the church to get real.
I decree that my past has an impact on the souls for the kingdom I have overcome by the word of my testimony in Jesus name.
I could not get myself together in my own strength it was the saving grace of Jesus that changed me.
I will not look down at those still suffering in the same sin I was in instead I will intercede for their deliverance in Jesus name.
I thank God I had a past.
I decree that my flesh will fight against me but the love I have for Jesus will keep me grounded.
I decree that there is nothing good coming from my flesh.
I decree that I will not let my flesh dictate to me in Jesus name.
If God delivered me from my past he can deliver me from the warfare in my future there are names attached to my future.
I declare that what I have done in my past I did out of ignorance. If you keep bringing my past up don't forget about the part about the redemption that took place in my life.
I decree that God has chosen me to conceive in Jesus name.

God did not give me a spirit of fear for the plans he has for my future.
I declare that I have to be ridiculed to be in the kingdom of God.
There is no shame to my game what I did I did I decree this in Jesus name.
I decree this is my season of preparation for the apostolic movement of God.
I declare that what is being birthed inside of me man can't take it away in Jesus name.
The degree of my character is greater than my gift. My character is going to be important in this movement for the kingdom of God.
What I did wrong was some else's right in Jesus name.
I decree that the anointing of God is taking me out of a messy situation.

Ruling in The Midst of My Enemy's

I decree that this is the hour that I must have the tongue of the learned in Jesus name.
I have the remnant of God surrounding me in this season I decree this in Jesus name.
God has turned everything the enemy thought was bad for me into the good in me.
I declare that I was one on the ones everybody said would not make but look what the Lord has done.
God requires me to speak from a learned tongue to reach his people.
I decree that my tongue is going to tell me what I have learned.
My enemies will no longer laugh at me in Jesus name.
Every weapon that was formed against me did not prosper the fire of God goes before me.
I decree that I'm hidden in the spiritual realm from demonic attacks in Jesus name.
The devil can no longer locate my prayers nor can he stop my prayers from being answered I declare this in Jesus name.
I declare that I'm coming out of survivor mood and moving into a conquering mood in Jesus name.
By surviving I have conquered the demons of my past the old has passed away in Jesus name.
I declare that I have a warfare mentality and the devil is defeated.
I know how to stay in the presence of God.
I decree that I may have been refused but I'm recognized.
The same people that rejected me will be the same ones that I will deliver in Jesus name.

I declare that I did not have religious rags when I was in my storm and I will not have religious rags now.
I curse every goliath spirit that has been holding me back from the fullness of God in Jesus name.
Every territorial spirit is broken and defeated in Jesus name.
I decree that God will use me to get the head demon and generational demon that has been ruling in my family in Jesus name.
I have tied the devils hands behind his back he has no effect over my bloodline in Jesus name.

Govern to Grace

I decree that when I did not know what to do the enabling grace of God allowed me to do his will.
God has enabled us with his grace in this season.
I declare that the enemy will never know the full plan and purpose that God has for my life.
God has already made provisions over my life there is no limit in Jesus name.
I decree that I will see myself the way God sees me.
Everything that is lying dormant in me God will breathe life onto it.
I declare that God will not give me an assignment without telling me what to do first. God has ordained me to reign and rule in Jesus name.
I will not let people define me I will be what God called me to be.
Father God I ask that you not only put your desires in my heart but also your vision in Jesus name.
I will put a demand on the grace of God in Jesus name.
God's grace and mercy has kept me this long and God will never give up on me.
I decree that God's grace and mercy has given me what I didn't deserve and kept me from getting what I do deserve in Jesus name.

Transformational Thinker

Transformational thinking has given me Godly thoughts in Jesus name.
I declare that my thought life has been transformed with the mind of Christ.
I decree that I will no longer reason in my mind in Jesus name.
Transformational thinking has me seeing into my apostolic future.
I see the greatness in all situations.

I decree that I will be around transformational thinkers like myself in Jesus name.
I will stay away from the wrong crowd they can block me from seeing and hearing God clearly in Jesus name.
My connection can be the cause of my cloudiness in Jesus name.
I will not be a dream killer caught in the mess of my past I decree this in Jesus name.
I curse and break every spirit of octopus mind control in Jesus name.
I declare that God won't take me past what I think God has given me a free will.
I refuse to let a gossiper's word become my thoughts I will not entertain any mess in my mind.
I decree that I will never stop seeing and believing in Jesus name.
I will free my mind from all ungodly soul ties of my past, present and future I decree this in Jesus name.
I declare that I will look at myself through the lens of God and see myself as he sees me.
God has already done a corporate evaluation and reformed minds in the body of Christ.
My thoughts will stay in the atmosphere of God.
I decree that I will not have any toxic thoughts against Gods will in Jesus name.
I will stay away from toxic saints that appear good on the outside but sour on the inside.
I declare that my mind is at peace in Jesus name.
I will not allow the toxic alliance of the enemy to leave residue on my mind in Jesus name.
Every trace of demonic venom has been erased off my mind by the word of God.
I release myself and my thought life from vampire people who only want to suck the life out of me in Jesus name.
I will not allow my spiritual man to die by dirty words I decree this in Jesus name.
I declare that all church hurt has been erased from my mind in Jesus name.
As a transformational thinker I am challenged with situations, circumstances, and purpose.

Who Am I

I am nothing without the grace and anointing of God.
Relational confirmation with Christ is the element I possess and display.
I ask myself can people see the Jesus in me.
I decree that I do display Jesus in my walk and talk.

I decree that I cannot think outside the will of God.
What flows out of my mouth is that which is in my heart in Jesus name.
I decree that my relationship is my conformation with God and the enemy desires to go after my relationship in Jesus name.
I am sealed in God the enemy cannot snatch me away or steal what God has for me.
I decree that I am a warrior, a conqueror, and a survivor and not a wimp the strongholds have been broken in Jesus name.
I declare that I a an end time warrior in Jesus name.

The Blood Over My Incarcerated Child

Father God in Jesus name I disarm all demonic forces, every deadly weapon formed against my son/daughter while incarcerated.
I decree that any spells of death and trickery all misfortune is released off my offspring in Jesus name.
I declare that my child will not be raped, or robbed of their innocence in Jesus name.
Father God I break every demonic cube and tear down the walls that tries to close my child in.
I curse every pattern of violence in my child's life I command all spiritual parasites, leaches, demonic worms and bugs will not take root into my child's mind or spirit in Jesus name.
Every infection of demonic activity is broken up into pieces and the blood of Jesus has made my child whole in Jesus name.
I command my son/daughters ears be closed to all demonic music, demonic poetry while incarcerated.
I curse every spirit of Ali (Muslim) I decree that no doctrines of devils will invade my child's atmosphere, I curse every spirit of Farrakhan and I bring confusion to the one trying to speak or influence my child into this lifestyle in Jesus name.
I declare that my son/daughter is a warrior for the one and only living Jesus Christ my child will spread the gospel of Jesus behind the prison walls in Jesus name.
I decree that my child will not have any demonic vision or purpose evil in their hearts.
By the blood of Jesus I free my son/daughter from the spirit of whoredom, abortion, and the homosexual nor lesbian spirit will not become attached to them behind prison walls in Jesus name.

I curse every spirit that will bear false witness against my seed.
The blood of Jesus will protect my child against the spirit of rape, incest, and molestation in Jesus name.
I curse every demonic prayer that enters my son/daughter atmosphere.
The blood of Jesus will protect my child from all gang violence behind bars in Jesus name.
I declare that my child will be safe from the spirit of conspiracy while behind bars in Jesus name.
I break and curse all jail house mentality my child has the mind of Christ.
My child is free from all bondage and spirits of rejection and self-rejection.
Father God my trust is in you to turn my child's life around release a spirit of salvation into every prison in Jesus name.
I curse every spirit of abandonment, loneliness, and neglect off my child.
I declare that my son/daughter will not have an idle mind for the devil to gain access to in Jesus name.
Father deliver my child from a spirit of stagnation; bring back every word of a God that they heard as a child create in my child a new and clean heart.
My child will be taught to be a man and women of God I declare this in Jesus name.
Holy Spirit reveal your spirit to my seed in Jesus name.
I thank you God for pushing their backs against the wall and getting their attention.
I cancel the assignment of all demonic confederations against my seed and I expose all their plans in Jesus name.
My son/daughter has the mind of Christ.
The blood of Jesus has saved my child from the fires of hell in Jesus name.
I curse all voices of darkness that torment my child I silence your voice in the name of Jesus.
The glory of God will shine on my son/daughter.
My child is victorious in Jesus name they are a living testimony for the kingdom.
I decree that the speed of God will refresh, renew, and restore my child in Jesus name.
Father God free my child from all demonic art, tattoos, and all literature from the underworld in Jesus name.
The fire of God will burn in my son/daughters spirit like never before in Jesus name.
The wrath of God will be released against all demons and the gates and plans of hell will not prevail against my child in Jesus name.

I'm God on Earth

I decree that my job on earth is to work as God for his apostolic kingdom.
I declare that the spiritual realm recognizes my voice I'm at a place of spiritual authority in Jesus name.
I want a fresh and new encounter with God the old just won't do.
Every day I tap into the greater one that lives on the inside of me in Jesus name.
I cannot put unclean hands on this move of God my hands are pure and my heart is clean I declare this in Jesus name.
I declare that as God releases a fresh move on earth everyone that has been desensitized will receive a fresh anointing like never before.
The old will not do we are in a fresh season there is nothing stale about the new move of God.
I will no longer feed my spirit with demonic worms Father forgive me from eating your word from the wrong table in Jesus name.
I decree that I walk in purity, holiness, and the righteousness of Jesus.
The enemy cannot paralyze my walk there are souls for the kingdom attached to me.
I answered the clarion call that is calling me to something greater than I have ever experienced.
I receive the fresh anointing, fresh oil, and the fresh glory of God.
I decree that I can't afford to flirt with my past to mess up my future I will not allow my past mistakes to keep me bound and from the God in me.
I declare that no voice will make me feel negative about what God is doing in my life.
I was born to be a transformer and I celebrate the assignment that God has given me.
I walk with the heartbeat of God.
I declare that the season of confirmation is over I will not waste time waiting t confirm what God already told me.
I know his voice and will move with his voice in Jesus name.
The word of God is being fulfilled in my generation I declare that in Jesus name.

Prophetic Atmosphere

God has given me the ability to hear his voice and I obey the voice of God.
I declare that the ministry of deliverance will open my eyes to the prophetic in Jesus name.

I will be obedient to the spirit of God and move when he tells me.
In decree that I will be innovated and creative in a prophetic atmosphere.
I desire the doorways to blessing in Jesus name.
I desire to hear the voice of God to be prophetic.
I decree that a prophetic atmosphere will uncover sin in Jesus name.
My desire is to be a prophet a mouth piece for this generation.
I declare that I am a prophetic (Elder, Minister, Apostle or Evangelist) in Jesus name.
I am a true servant for the Lord.
For these are the days of true restoration Father God I ask that you pour your spirit upon all flesh and blood.
I decree that first I must be delivered from a religious spirit before I can go any further in Christ I will be a true Apostle for the kingdom.
I live my life in surrendered obedience in Jesus name.
I live every day with God I have a heavy pursuit for the spiritual gifts from of God.
I decree that my gifts are to bless the nations in Jesus name.
I will not be selective on who I use my gifts on.
I declare that God is doing me a favor by using me as a chosen vessel in Jesus name.
I will always stay in a place of humility in Jesus name.
I decree that I will not allow other people to control me with their gifts.
I may have to prophesize to my enemy in Jesus name by me praying for my enemy will break their hearts of stone.
I declare that I will not be afraid to use the gifts that God has given me.
I declare that I'm flowing in my now season in Jesus name.
I have the healing gift of faith in Jesus name.
I decree that I will not be stuck in a Pentecostal mindset I will walk with authority, maturity and purpose.
I declare that the Bishop movement has damaged the church in Jesus name.
I cannot be apostolic and kingdom minded and follow the catholic religion I follow the doctrine of Jesus Christ.
I have 20/20 eyesight I'm a sniper in the realm of the spirit I decree this in Jesus name.
I decree that I will not be unlearned and religious in this season.
I refuse to give away what Christ paid for, for the sake of man's honor.
I declare that the spirit of God desires to use everyone.
I need the Holy Spirit to make it here on earth.
I must stay in present day truth in my prophetic atmosphere.
I can never take a risk for God and be disappointed in Jesus name.
I want to call on the beauty of God.
I decree that my yokes were destroyed because of the anointing of Jesus.

I declare that in my present day the manifest presence of God comes to meet me needs.
The presence of God lifts the burden off of my life.
I decree that a prophetic mantle was released over my life.
I speak through the vein of God.
I will not condemn myself for misinterpreting what God has said.
I will move in faith I will accelerate with my gifts.
I repent for quenching and grieving the Holy Spirit in Jesus name.
God I ask that you reveal to me the imposters in the kingdom.
Jesus told me to do greater works.
I decree that apostolic people stay grounded and connected to the heart of God.
I declare that no religious demon will get the glory for what God has done in my life.
I will cast out devils in others and myself in Jesus name.
I will break the strategies of satan and I will violently take control of the kingdom of God.
I decree that "Thy kingdom come in earth" breaks demonic force.
God commands me to have a prophetic lifestyle in Jesus name.

I Must Qualify the People Around Me

I declare that I have a kingdom schedule and have no time for other people to drop their mess on me.
I have a lot of visibility and God will use me very powerful for kingdom work.
In this season God is cross pollenating God's agenda is bigger than mine would ever be.
I decree that people who are in my circle have the expression of Jesus all over them in Jesus name.
I decree that this apostolic movement is liberal there is nothing denominational about it.
I will not make a denomination an idol in my life.
I decree that I will not allow my friends to keep me bound in Jesus name.
I refuse to stay in a place of hurt and bitterness and I will not allow anyone who carries those spirits to be around me.
I decree that I will obey God and come into my fullness in Jesus name.
I will only accept a title if I can walk in the apostolic with it.
I will not allow anyone around me that try to contaminate the move of God I decree this in Jesus name.

My clergy collar doesn't make me an apostle in Jesus name.
I will not allow my friends to bring junk from religion into the apostolic.
I decree that apostolic people are trend setters in Jesus name.
Father God I ask that you cleanse my mind from things that I learned that was not the truth.
I decree that I will listen to the spirit of truth in Jesus name.
The word tells me that I can't advance the kingdom from a stale revelation I will advance the kingdom with present day truth in Jesus name.
When I connect with the correct people we all can advance the kingdom.
I break the spirit of being embarrassed when God blesses me in Jesus name.
I decree that I will not allow my friends to attack who I am in Christ.
I'm going to embrace the grace of God.
I will deal with people who celebrate me and not just tolerate me in Jesus name.
If you were not with me in the valley you do not qualify to be with me in the kingdom.
I will not operate in procrastination which is a spirit of rebellion.
I decree that I will not let people keep me in a box.
God has given me a kingdom connection that will last in Jesus name.
I declare that I will be with people who can speak into my mow and destiny.
I decree that I will not hang with seasonal people who change churches every sixty days.
I declare that I will not change my covenant like I change my underwear.
The season is over for two-face people to be in my life in Jesus name.
I value my kingdom covenants.
I'm letting go of all the folks I can't take into my next season they heard the same word but did not move.
I wash my hands from all counterfeit people in my life.
From this day on I decree that all my friends must be kingdom minded.
I decree that God has set me over the nations.
My advancement is going to come from kingdom minded people.
Father God I ask you from this day forward that you only allow me to be with kingdom mined, strong covenant relational people I declare this in the might name of Jesus
I can't hang with people who agree with sin this will desensitize my relationship with God I paid too much for this anointing that I carry in Jesus name.
The word tells me to know them that labor among you.
I declare that a true covenant friend will never let me give up.

Gateway Churches

I declare that in this season God is going to allow heaven to invade earth God's righteousness, his majesty, and the holiness of God will dwell among us.
I decree that my church will release the presence and anointing of God in Jesus name.
God will use me as a chosen vessel in Jesus name.
I shall put no wicked things before my eyes so evil will not be established in my heart.
I will read and discover the revelation of the doctrine of Christ in Jesus name.
I decree that I will not allow my ears to hear the doctrines and words of devils in Jesus name.
There will not be anything that I have heard or seen that will bring a spirit of fear inside of me.
I decree that whatever I give my ear to that is what I will become in Jesus name.
I will not be deceived by the devil and his army I decree this in Jesus name.
I bind every spirit of perversion and pornography off the body of Christ.
I will guard every personal gateway in my life in Jesus name.
Father God forgive me a shedding blood by allow my body to be tattooed in Jesus name.
I cancel the assignment of the demonic eye that is tattoo on my back I will no longer allow satan access to me in Jesus name.
I declare that you cannot turn anything demonic into the apostolic or prophetic.
I bind every hand that tries this in the kingdom of God.
I renounce every tattoo out of ignorance I confess that Jesus is Lord over my life in Jesus name.
I need to be delivered and set free from any and all covenants I made with demons that try to block my gateways in Jesus name.
Father God show me what I gave access to that are still demonic covenants in my life.
I curse every demon effecting my character in Jesus name I will not have any flaws in my character.
God does not mix a truth and a lie in Jesus name.
Every lie that I have lied under and believed I curse it in Jesus name.
I declare that my personal gateway must remain clean I refuse to listen to anyone mess in Jesus name.
My personal gates will remain pure and clean to send off a pure sound of the heavens in Jesus name.

I decree that I will not allow my gates to be torn down by negativity this will only tear me up on the inside.
As long as my heart is clean my gateway will be pure.
God flows through me by my pure gateway I decree this in Jesus name.
I command all pastors, and leader to be gatekeepers of the apostolic truth and wisdom in Jesus name.
I decree that I will be pure in my teaching of God's word.
I will not flood my gateways with demonic thinking in Jesus name.
I call forth every leaders spirit into obedience that they will preach the truth and not be afraid of losing members or tithes in Jesus name.
I will not step out of the order of the kingdom of God if I do so I will lose my anointing in Jesus name.
I decree that I will not tap into a realm that is not the sound of God.
God is calling forth all gatekeepers to take there post in Jesus name.
I decree that demonic confederacies have no entry into my gateway.
I declare that me being a gatekeeper makes me harmless as a dove.
I decree that all churches must be built on the foundation of the word.
I decree that I will allow the Holy Spirit to discern what people tell me in Jesus name.
I decree that all gateway churches should have angels descending and ascending.
I repent for not doing what I was called to do in the kingdom of God.
I declare that my church is an epicenter deploying the people of God into his army.
I am the gateway to heaven I'm the only bible some people will ever see.
I decree there is no draw backs in this season witches and warlocks are waiting for us to get off to gain access in Jesus name.
I declare that my church carries a tangible anointing in Jesus name.
As a gatekeeper I prevent uncleanness from entering my city, I send a warning in the spiritual realm in Jesus name.
My church binds the works of darkness from my city, region, and nation.
When I put a demand on the anointing the preacher and teacher will have to shift in Jesus name.
I declare that all gateway churches becomes river in the dry dessert in Jesus name we will water the earth spiritually.
I am the river here on earth in the dry places; my rivers stay fresh with the word of God.
I decree that I possess the gates of the enemy in Jesus name.

I'm Walking in A Season Of No Drawbacks

I decree that violence should not be greater than the voice of God.
I declare that in this season I will not use my weakness as s religious excuse as to why I'm not going forward.
I carry a tangible anointing in Jesus name.
I will not settle for any demonic thoughts that try to pull me back into my forgiven past.
I will not settle for a weak anointing in Jesus name.
I declare that I will not put my assignment down because people hate to see me move forward I will not lose my momentum for anyone.
I have been empowered to deal with the demons and devils from my past.
My God is a progressive God I'm growing in leaps in Jesus name.
In this season I declare that I will not sit under any dead leaders I'm all about my father business.
I decree that where there is a demand God will supply.
I'm leaving church with my eyes open to see and my ears open to hear the word of God and truth.
God I need and encounter with you like never before.
I declare that every weapon and vessel that has been assigned to me to pull my backwards I break your grip on my life in Jesus name.
God I have to be empowered by you.
The hand of God keeps me from going backwards.
I decree there is nothing good in my past and if there is anything that God wants me to have from my past he will bring it to me I don't have to go looking for it.
This is the season that I ask myself how bad do I want the anointing.
I put a demand on the grace of God.
At church I am healed and delivered and set free in Jesus name.
I declare that we are not just a church but a movement from God.
I decree that my hunger for God can make me preach his word.
I have no regrets about my past mistakes I have been forgiven and made whole in Jesus name.
Father God I ask that you wrap me in your glory and never let go.
In this season I have a great responsibility I declare this in Jesus name.
I'm covered in the blood I can never go back to my yesterdays.
I decree that what I speak is part of who I am in Jesus name.
I decree that I will not feed his sheep stale bread but I will feed them daily bread.
I declare that it is God that keeps me from falling I'm at that place in him.
I must download the patience of God.

Before I tell anyone else I must apply it to myself in Jesus name.
I decree that accountability will come back to the body and leaders of Christ.
The kingdom is where ever I go it is inside of me.
I decree that God has delivered me from a costume spirit one way at church and another way at home.
I declare that my heart must be pure to be an open channel there can be no jealousy, strife, anger, bitterness, or envy in Jesus name.
I will let the old revelation go and God will give me a new fullness of present day truth I declare thisi n Jesus name.
I know the will of the Lord for me and my family.

Manifesting Prophetic Purpose

I decree that I Cleary have sight of understanding in Jesus name.
I decree that there is purpose for me pain my pain is for my gain.
Before I die everything that God has spoken over me shall come to pass.
I declare that in the other side of my pain there is possibility and potential.
My pain built new character inside of me God used my pain to bring the mess out of me.
I will perform all the word that was spoken over me in Jesus name.
I decree there is a heavenly plan and purpose for my life I didn't go through it for nothing.
I declare that every mistake that I have made God is going to turn it around and make a miracle out of it.
My prophetic purpose may have been detoured but it has not been denied I decree this in Jesus name.
My purpose is to discover and develop what God already has spoken over my life.
I declare it is not my decision but my discovery.
My private victory always displays public praise.
The favor of God over my life brings jealousy that people don't understand my anointing or call.
I will watch what I tell people in Jesus name.
Because I walk in the favor of God he reveals deep things to me I decree this in Jesus name.
I'm waiting patiently on the word that was spoken over my life.
I declare that God is sending his word to where I am at in my life.
I decree that God will keep his promise towards me.

God word found me right where I was (crack house, jail, and bar) and I thank God for finding me.
God has given me the option to gain back my authority in Jesus name.
I declare that I was called not to follow the trend but be a trend setter for people to follow.
I have an anointing to get the ball rolling for the kingdom of God.
I decree that I am an apostolic trailblazer a front runner to establish the present day truth to the body of Christ.
I have a supernatural release for the kingdom of God.
I declare that my God given endurance will keep me standing in the day of battle.
I will not allow a church to limit the move of God for my life.
I decree that I will not allow a spirit of bitterness to root in my life to turn into cancer in Jesus name.
God is using me as a pattern to show his children how to go through longsuffering in Jesus name.
I declare that I won't blame God for what I'm going through.
I am a well for God the living water runs out of me and the devil can't stop this living water I decree this in Jesus name.
God has released me from all mental anguish and torment.
I decree that I will not be a saint and live under a curse.
God gave me the present-day revelation for the body of Christ.
I'm called to break vicious cycle of demonic principalities in the heavenly.
I decree that war defines apostolic ministry.

Deep Sea Fishing

I declare that in this season I will launch out into the deep.
I'm called to go deep into the cities to pray.
I decree that I will stop wasting time on souls that don't want to change.
In this day I declare that the deeper the sin the deeper the consequences.
The more I stay in the presence of God the deeper his thoughts become mine.
I decree that I will find my deep place in God for the deliverance of my family in Jesus name.
The deeper my walk is with God the deeper my concentration will be.
I decree that I will launch out into the deep to reach souls in crack houses, bars, clubs, sexual sins, and violence the ones nobody wants to reach.
I cannot have a spirit of fear in this season I will walk in the boldness of Jesus Christ.

I decree that I'm coming up against all negativity directed towards me.
I'm so far out in the deep the devil cannot locate me; the devil can't pick me up in my prayers I decree this in Jesus name.
I declare that my mouth will speak into the deep and bring in souls that are thirsty for God.
In my deep sea fishing there is going to be great deliverance threw out the land I decree this in Jesus name.
My deep sea fishing has silenced the voice of the enemy in Jesus name.
I decree that I will unearth the revelation knowledge of God's word and teach it to the nations in Jesus name.
Every mystery will be revealed to me in this season.
I declare that I will not speak from a dark perspective in Jesus name.
While I am in the deep I will not let my own words smear me in Jesus name.
No trap or snare of the devil can stop me in the deepness of God.
I decree that all human devils will not follow me into the deep.
My light is shining brighter than bright in Jesus name.
In my deep season no lie spoken about me shall come to pass in Jesus name.
My mouth is lined up with the move of God.
In this deep season people are drawn to my anointing I declare this in Jesus name.
There is no time for repenting over the same issues in this season it's time to walk in maturity I declare this in Jesus name.
God has already predestined me for greatness and I claim it in Jesus name.
God already attached my assignment for deep sea fishing I grabbed and it and holding on to it in Jesus name.
I apostolically release a spirit of faith, wisdom, revelation, grace supplication, and longsuffering in Jesus name.
I release the spirit of Jehu over the body of Christ in Jesus name.

Amalekites Spirits

Father God in Jesus name I cancel every spirit of falsehood, and I ask that every person with a hidden agenda be exposed, remove all the busy bodies from the pull pits and congregation. I cancel the assignment of all spirits of Hittites that try to force fear and terror on the body of Christ. I curse every spirit of Jebusites that promotes gossip, slander, always putting down people and coming against the leaders in the church only to bring confusion. I curse every spirit of Ammorite that brings pride into a church, always wanting to be noticed, I curse the spirit of self-glory and promotion in Jesus name. I curse every pedestal spirit in Jesus name. Father we come up against all Canaanites spirits that always tells you to do the wrong thing and tempt you in Jesus name.

Gods Prophecy

I declare that prophecy is the voice of God his thoughts and his ways and I receive it and obey it in Jesus name.
I decree that God is helping me through all the doors he has opened for me.
God did not speak over my life just for the fun of it.
I will declare what God is saying in Jesus name.
I'm in my season that I think like God and have the mind of Christ.
I receive all the downloads from heaven.
God's prophecy has pulled me from my past and walked me into my future.
I decree that God has made me of value and worth.
I value prophetic ministry in Jesus name.
I seek after prophetic thoughts and move in a prophetic direction in Jesus name.
God has empowered me to impact the world.
I decree that my prophetic word has creative ability in Jesus name.
I declare that fulfillment is looking for me.

Dung Gate

In Jesus name I release the Dung gate spirit on the body of Christ with this anointing we will bring great deliverance into the kingdom and on the streets of cities, and the region where we dwell.
We will be able to go into the dark places and cast out devils, and bring deliverance to those still in bondage.
There will be a separation for sanctification in Jesus name.
We will not only stand strong and in unity but we will be detached from everything demonic.
I silence the voice of the accuser in Jesus name.
I command every principality to be broken off the regions, cities, and nations.
I decree that I am destined to bring deliverance and be apostolically rooted in Jesus name.

I cancel the vagabond spirit off the body of Christ I command that your spirit will be settled at one church for the kingdom in Jesus name.
I declare that I am radical, ready and redeem for apostolic kingdom work.
My mentality is all about my father business in Jesus name.

What God Says for This Season

In this season we must bring forth a new praise like never before.
For those of us that held on God is going to give us a new strength we are his remnants.
God is releasing a spirit of radicalness upon the body.
God desire for us in this season is to penetrate into new realms spiritually.
God is requiring his people to come to a place of commitment, clarity, and faithfulness.
In this season there is no room for excuses.
God is going to use our worship to penetrate demonic principalities over nations.
God is going to smother every sickness in our bodies with his glory.
Our praise has to come out in full measure so it will break the walls and strongholds that are holding some people back.
We also have to come up in our prayer life no more microwave prayers.
Something's that are going on in our life is because we have not snatched it in the spirit.
God is about to take us out of our bodies to another realm spiritually.
We are to penetrate in our giving tithing is a worship relationship.
God is going to shoot us in the spirit to see things that we can't see with are natural eye then come back to our natural to pray against what the enemy's plans are.
We are to listen to the sounds of the winds a catching in the spirit that we can shift with the word of God.
The enemy will have a hard time trying to locate us in this season.
We have to shift on the same tune as one unified body be on one accord.
God wants us to know that heaven is living inside of us.
God wants us to go up so he can come down.
A command is coming to our spirits to remove laziness to bring forth our gifts that are lying dormant.

Anointed to Destroy and Pull Down

I cancel the assignment of the spirit of Hosheik and break the cloud of darkness assigned to my area in Jesus name.
I declare that I am the light in my region.
In Jesus name I decree that the enemy is afraid of the backlash against his kingdom he doesn't want me to realize how powerful my voice is.
What I proclaim shall happen in Jesus name.
I'm expecting the fulfillment that God has promised to be released on the body of Christ.
In Jesus name I release a Cyrus anointing to fall among the people of God.
With my Cyrus anointing I can speak to the storms of life and all demonic winds.
I have dominion over the land I am a ruler for the kingdom I have ownership I declare this in Jesus name.
I understand that my authority is no good without dominion.
I decree that my right hand is a symbol of authority and righteousness in Jesus name.
I decree that I need dominion to stay delivered.
I will preach to the demonic spirits and not people.
My anointing has nothing to do with church as normal I'm at a new level in Jesus name.
My anointing will settle issues in my heart and mind; my anointing will bring me into a new place of maturity.
I decree that God gave me the power to say satan the Lord rebukes thee.
I decree that every time I open my mouth the devil shakes in Jesus name.
My presence confounds the enemy when he looks at me he sees what he had now he see Jesus when he looks at me I decree this in Jesus name.
I'm made of pure beauty the ugliness of sin has been washed away in Jesus name.

Fruit of an Apostolic House

I decree that we are sent by God in this season.
We carry a global mandate for the kingdom.
I declare there is no time for dead fruit anything that will not grow or prosper God will remove.
God is expecting good fruit to spring forth from us in Jesus name.

I declare that if the church you belong to is not pure you will not have any roots for kingdom work.

I received my impartation and I will go forward and produce new fruits in Jesus name.

I decree that my first fruits has released streams of sweet water and brought me a refreshing.

I shall not have any bitter water flowing out of me.

I declare that there in my apostolic church there is a sweet aroma in Jesus name.

I declare that as a leader my spirit reflects the image of Jesus.

I can't straddle the fence with sin and be apostolic.

God I ask that you exposé and deliver me from all bad fruit.

I decree that demons should not be able to sit in my presence and be comfortable in Jesus name.

I declare that I cannot speak in tongues than cuss my brother or sister out, and walk by people and don't speak in Jesus name.

I decree I won't put the Holy Spirit on the shelf and purposely sin in Jesus name.

I won't play the card "God knows my heart" and end of in a devil's hell.

I declare that as an apostolic person I will guard my tongue and watch what I say and respond to in Jesus name.

I decree that my anointing will allow me to talk to and pray for those that talk against me in Jesus name.

I thank God for holiness my pure anointing will bring change.

I declare that I am a light and a beacon of hope in Jesus name.

I receive my influence from God I decree this in Jesus name.

Because I am apostolic when I turn on the lights the roaches (demons) will run.

The light of Jesus illuminates me I decree this in Jesus name.

I curse the spirit of Skotta and remove its dark covering and heaviness off the body of Christ in Jesus name.

I'm called to preserve the word and moves of God I will keep them alive, and make it last.

I decree that I was called to be the salt to my region God has delegated me to go forth in Jesus name.

My destiny was not my decision it was my discovery I declare this in Jesus name.

God marked my pathway from the beginning of time in Jesus name.

I decree that I'm a preserver of holiness, righteousness, and integrity where ever I go.

I'm sent to go forth in the name Jesus not on my behalf.

I understand that I'm not here because I am perfect but I here because of Jesus.
I decree that I can handle all darkness in Jesus name.
I declare that God's apostolic presence must come out of my countenance in Jesus name.
There will be places that God will send me and tell me not to open my mouth it will be his presence in me that will bring about deliverance/change I declare this in Jesus name.
When I show up the countenance of God appears and this brings confusion to my enemy's.
I decree that I will not lose my look of authority in Jesus name.
I dare the devil or his demons to show up I have an apostolic countenance in Jesus name.
I declare I have the glow of Jesus in my countenance.
God apostolic presence will cause me to perform in Jesus name.
I carry what the world is thirsting for.
The light inside of me will save my offspring, grandchildren and my generation I declare this in Jesus name.
God has put his foot down about that what concerns me that's why the devil is so mad.

My Election For Repentance

I declare that Gods blood is stronger than any sin I was in.
God made me a new creature when he came into my life.
I declare that when the devil reminds me of my past I remind him of future.
I decree that the devil can't kill me because I was elected and chosen.
I am sure of my election in Christ.
I decree that my promotion is right at my fingertips God is about to give me more than I ever had.
I received my new fire from God.
I'm getting ready to go higher in God I will not get discouraged I thank all my haters for talking about me and lying on me.
I decree that the devil is afraid of my promotion in Jesus name.
I declare that the hell that I am in cannot destroy me look at the hell I came out of.
I will still keep my focus on God while my enemies still tries to attack me.
I decree that God will prepare a table in the presence of my enemies for me.

The Cross I Bare

I declare that an apostolic house produces cross bearers in Jesus name.
I'm called to crucify my flesh and to bring the nation to its knees in Jesus name.
I decree that the cross is the power of God to those that are saved.
My life represents the cross in Jesus name.
I will not idolize the cross I will believe in the redemption power that took place.
I decree that we have to identify with the cross in Jesus name.
I decree that the cross represents the pain, sorrow, and shame I had to deal with.
I am satisfied not to be with the in crowd in Jesus name.
I will not allow a spirit of rejection to block me from where God wants me to go.
I decree that a spirit of rejection will not taint my anointing in Jesus name.
I declare that no demon can stand up against my preaching.
If I take everything personal I am not a cross bearer in Jesus name.
The rejection qualified me to be called to preach apostolically.
I'm sent in the name of Jesus.
I decree that I will not reject a person's anointing in Jesus name.
I'm being used because of God's grace.
I declare that in this season God is raising up the one who people counted out in Jesus name.
I had to be humiliated and ridiculed to pass my test.
I decree that my anointing is seen in the spiritual realm.
I have taken up the cross in Jesus name.
The devil is afraid of my spiritual authority in Jesus name.
I declare that I can't start a church out of being hurt before I stand before Gods people and preach I have to make sure my spirit is right in Jesus name.
Jesus does not have to bear the cross alone I have to die to my personal sin and my flesh in Jesus name.
I decree that dying to my flesh will stop me from fornicating, adultery, masturbating, lying and cheating in Jesus name.
I decree that the cross is just not an emblem that I wear.
I refuse to let the devil take me back to where I used to be in Jesus name.
I decree that I have to be real to myself in Jesus name.
I will not play with sin and put confidence in my flesh.
I decree that I will not compromise with sin in Jesus name.
I declare that after all the offenses I did to Jesus I have no right to be offended in Jesus name.

I will sharpen the gifts that God has given me in Jesus name.
I decree that I don't have the "I" syndrome when I am a cross bearer.
I declare that my maturity will help me restore my brother or sister I can pick up their pain in the spiritual realm in Jesus name.
I decree that I can't be called to ministry and not feel others pain.
I declare that my anointing is not for me but the people in Jesus name.
Christ delivered me from the world and the power of Satan in Jesus name.

My Haters

I declare that my haters are mad that God is using me and they are questioning God.
God has broken through tradition because of the plans he has for my life in Jesus name.
I decree that I have a word from the Lord that is why he raised me up.
I will remember the word of God and not what people are saying about me.
The word of God flows out of my mouth and my haters can't twist the word.
I decree that I will not let fear set into my spirit in Jesus name.
My supply does not come from my haters but from God.
My haters are jealous of the word inside of me that can change a region in Jesus name.
I declare that God is going to prove himself faithful in my life.
I renounce every spirit of unbelief in Jesus name.
God is letting my haters hang on so they can see his glory come to past in my life.
I decree that every church needs haters to survive.
I declare that I will guard what God has said in Jesus name.
I decree that I have to be a watchman in the spiritual realm.
I declare there is prosperity in my mouth.
God through his word into the earth and I am the wide receiver who caught it in Jesus name.
My haters hate the fact that I am a solider in the army of the Lord and they are just bystanders.
My haters hate the glow of God that shines on my outside.
In Jesus name I will pray for all my haters what God has done for me he can do for them I declare this in Jesus name.
I declare that I will give my haters direction and show them the love of Christ.
I will teach my haters how to go into the presence of God and be set free from jealousy in Jesus name.

I declare that I will not spiritual die by the hands of my haters I will die for changing a region and nation.
It don't matter what my family, friends, and church people think about me my walk is pleasing to God.
I won't believe the lies of my haters they only want me to go as far as they want me to and have only what they think I should have.
God have mercy on my haters in Jesus name.
I decree that all I need is my faith I God to run the race.

Keeper Of the Flame

The fire of God burns strongly with in us God allows us to carry his flame I decree this in Jesus name.
I declare that the flames are going to bring healing, deliverance and a fresh anointing into my life.
I decree that the miracle of God already lives on the inside of me.
I have accepted the responsibility of the Holy Spirit this will keep my flame burning in I declare this in Jesus name.
I will guard my flame by watching what I hear and what I say in Jesus name.
I decree that being a gossiper will make my flame go out.
I am a gatekeeper of the flame of God I declare that in Jesus name.
I cannot go to the nations without my flame burning full force.
I decree that God has dealt with the mess inside of me before he built my ministry.
I declare that God dealt with my character so my flame would not go dim.
I will not blaspheme the Holy Spirit by going into bars; drugs, fornicating, and adultery then come to church like nothing is wrong I decree this in Jesus name.
I declare that my ministry will die without the fire of God.
By me going to the nations is all about souls and not glorifying my name.
I declare that I will take authority and be a keeper of the flames.
Whoever I trust is the one that will change my destiny I decree this in Jesus name.
I decree that I will only walk with people of destiny, wisdom and integrity.
I will not allow a spirit of rejection to kill my flame I declare this in Jesus name.
I will die daily to my fleshly desires to keep my flame from becoming dull.
I will always speak present day truth there are souls involved I decree this in Jesus name.

God is my light and I and his word is wrapped around me.
My flame is going to save the world I decree this in Jesus name.
I decree that I will not be addicted to a love that is not God.
The more word I have inside of me the stronger my sword will be.
I cannot do spiritual warfare if I'm not skilled at it I must stay connected to God by his flame.
I decree that I shall pierce the darkness with my sword and flame of God.
I will daily remind the devil that I'm a keeper of the flame and my anointing is stronger than ever. I decree this in Jesus name.
The grace of God will carry me through all persecution.
I must keep my heart pure and my fire pure to go before God.
My flame is preparing me for when I go home to be with Jesus.

Gods Glory Shall Return

I declare that these are days of distinction we are set apart.
Just like the Ark of the Covenant I will walk in governmental authority and with the presence of God I declare this in Jesus name.
I decree that the things of God will teach me his voice and sprit.
I will always praise God for his glory returning to the churches.
I declare that the prophecy spoken over my life will not be revoked heaven will never reject me in Jesus name.
I declare that I will pray for all my loved ones that God is displeased with in Jesus name.
I will cast out all demons of drama, and trouble that our in my way I will not counsel a demon but cast him out in Jesus name.
I'm concerned about the glory of God over my church.
I declare that the glory of God will remove all false leaders from the pulpits in Jesus name.
I decree that I will not allow an religious spirit to seduce me into the ways of man/.
I ask God to restore our allegiance to him and not man.
Real leadership will pioneer me into my destiny in Jesus name.
I decree that signs of God's glory are shown in the way I have changed.
I will pray and fast to bring God's glory back to the church I decree this in Jesus name.
I declare that the glory of God is changing leadership all around the earth.
God is not going to compromise his holiness for me or no one else.

Spirit of Elijah

I release a spirit of Elijah over the body of Christ to symbolize what God wants done in his church.
I will decree & declare what I want to be accomplished into the spiritual realm.
I declare that Gods house will once again become a place of prayer in Jesus name.
I will remove everything that God sees wrong and reveals to me in Jesus name.
I declare that an apostolic house shall release the full spirit of prayer in Jesus name.
I decree that my house is that secret and intimate place that shows God who I am.
Father God I invite you to my house to remove any and everything that is pulling me away from being a house of prayer in Jesus name.
I decree that there will be a block on every one that wants to steal or pimp my anointing in Jesus name.
I declare that I am a house of the Lord.
I decree that my prayer life has tapped into a new realm in Jesus name.
I can't bless a nation until I bless myself in Jesus name.
My spirit of prayer will allow God to lay his head down and dwell with me.
I decree that my prayer life will make a liar out of the devil in Jesus name.
Just as Elijah did I will speak it and it will come to pass.

Soulish Prophecy

Father I cancel the assignment of all Soulish prophecy spoken over my life I command that word to be void of life, to have no meaning and I return it to the sender in Jesus name.
I decree that I will not hang around with people who try to help the enemy destroy my life through words.
I declare that I will open my ears to hear from the spiritual realm.
My outward appearance reflects the outward appearance of God I decree this in Jesus name.
I declare that my spirit came from the inbreathed breath of God.
I decree that I will teach my soul to say I will in Jesus name.
When I walk in disobedience I'm killing my soul so Father God I repent from walking in disobedience in Jesus name.

I decree that the rebel inside of me must be put to death.
Father God expose every demonic voice that tries to speak into my life. By the blood of Jesus I silence the voice of the enemy in Jesus name.
Every demonic prophecy that I have received I command you to come out of my spirit in Jesus name.
I decree that it was my new birth that brought me back to life.
I will not allow my body to be corruptible in Jesus name.
Thank you God for resurrecting and enthroning me.
My soul through repentance is reconciled to God.
I renounce every spirit of rebellion that would have me believe and listen to Soulish prophecy in Jesus name.
I will not use prophecy just to be seen or speak what God did not say in Jesus name.
I refuse to allow Soulish prophecy to talk me out of my blessing in Jesus name.
I decree that I have an inner reality of Christ.
I decree that my spirit is capable of direct communication with God.
I declare that my spirit originated from God and I can fellowship with him through prayer and worship.
I command every witch and warlock to be exposed that come to my church to plant and release soulish prophecy in Jesus name.
God please expose any charismatic person in the congregation that refuses to submit to Godly leadership.
I decree that I will not use personal prophecy to attract people in Jesus name.
Father God I ask that you break every counterfeit prophecy that is going out across the air waves, television, and radio in Jesus name.
I command that the mouths of those trying to speak lies into my life be confused in Jesus name.
I cancel the assignment of church hoppers who go around from church to church giving out parking lot prophecy in Jesus name.
I stop all soulish prophecy from stopping people from coming to church in Jesus name.
I break the sting of all demonic words spoken over my life in Jesus name.
I cancel the spirit of self-glory thinking every platform should be about me in Jesus name.
I command every spirit in the pull pits that's all about self-glory to go to the pits of hell in Jesus name.
I expose all organized witchcraft that sends out witches and warlocks that deliberately subvert, manipulate, and destroy churches I plead the blood of Jesus against you and cancel your assignment in Jesus name.

Father God I ask that you destroy all dummy churches run by witches and warlocks that purposely pervert your word in Jesus name.
I will pray and stand in the gap for all those that give out Soulish prophecy in Jesus name.
I declare that I will not pray in agreement with satan desires in Jesus name.
I cancel the spirit of Divination the false gift of prophecy in Jesus name.
I declare that just because it is spiritual and happens in the church, does not mean that it is from God.
I curse the spirit behind Christian Fantasy and Fables, Christian Tradition and Clichés Soulish Prophecy, Spiritual Adultery, False Gifts and Fruits, Jezebel, Ahab, Rebellion, bastard spirit, double minded hatred for true prophets of God, spirit that wants to be seen and heard, attitude of weakness, bruised hearts, bruised minds false anointing in Jesus name.
I declare that a soulish mind-set influences every area of my life.

My Prayer Life

I decree that a steady prayer life will keep me in communion with God.
I declare that prayer allows me to hear what is happening in the heavenlies.
I will do what Gods heart desires by praying his will on earth what is in the heavenlies.
I decree that when we release the sound of God with our voices on in the earth realm the enemy trembles with fear.
I declare I will not let a spirit of religion destroy my prayer life.
My pray life is the life line to my visions coming to past I decree this in Jesus name.
I decree that my prayers will release the mandate of God into his kingdom.
My spirit is always positioned to pray in Jesus name.
I live my life like every day is my last day to fellowship with God.
I decree that I will not block my prayers by being wrapped up in sin.
All the struggles I face come from a lack of prayer in Jesus name.
I declare that my prayers have an assignment to bring forth the assignments of God.
I declare that my prayers will not lay dormant in Jesus name.
I allow God to download his word into my life.
I will not be in a dangerous place to do things for God without a prayer life.
I will allow a spirit of prayer to be released into me.
My prayers help me stay in Gods zone in Jesus name.
I will not give heed to the devils tricks to keep me from praying in Jesus name.

I decree that church is not a substitute for prayer.
I carry the nations in my spirit and I need prayer I decree this in Jesus name.
God allowed me to go through so I can go to the nations.
I decree that my prayer life is fully developed from the inside and out.
I declare that God choose me to prayer for those who are still stuck in the sin that I was delivered from.
I will allow God to shift me in prayer.
I declare that the explosive power of God is being released in my life through prayer.
I'm being sheppard into the things of God.

Elected for Promotion

God I ask that you remove and take away anything that is hindering me from my new season that I am in.
I will not believe the lies of the devil that will have me believe that this is not my season.
God has taught me how to walk softly and stand my ground in this new season I decree this in Jesus name.
This is my season of great and everlasting breakthrough in Jesus name.
I decree that this is a great season of warfare in Jesus name.
I will not believe the devils misconception that the word I preach has no affect and nothing will happen.
I thank God for his grace allowing me to get things right in Jesus name.
The devil is attacking me in my new season because of my promotion in Jesus name.
I declare that I was one of the ones that everybody thought would not go anywhere in life but look what the Lord has done.
I am part of the remnant of God his spirit goes where ever I go in Jesus name.
I decree that the enemy wants to disqualify me but God is using it to qualify me.
I waited patiently to be elected in Jesus name.
I have God's grace and unmerited favor in Jesus name.
I decree that I am what I am by the grace of God man wanted to count me out in Jesus name.
There is not anything man can do to stop what God has elected I decree this in Jesus name.

I thank people who threw dirt on me I am a seed of God and the dirt helped me grow in Jesus name.
The dirt made me understand I am the remnant of God.
God has handpicked me out of the body of Christ to use me in this season.

Religion Has No Place in Apostolic

I declare that Jesus is speaking to the religious system.
My life must stay in the will of God I decree this in Jesus name.
I walk in present day truth not the truth of the religious system.
I decree that I will not reject the mindset of God.
I declare that I have a grace gift in Jesus name.
I declare that the Holy Spirit is coming after every paradigm that comes from a religious system.
My apostolic mindset is called to judge the religious system I decree this in Jesus name.
I decree that I live a holy lifestyle because of my fear and respect for God.
I will do as Jesus did and preach the kingdom of God.
I will not allow a religious system to shut my mouth in Jesus name.
I cancel the assignment of every religious person that tries to fight against my God given authority.
With my apostolic mindset I believe everyone should be free in Jesus name.
I decree that God will back up the word that I teach in Jesus name.
My praise has a spiritual revelation that breaks through any religious system.
As an apostolic person I would rather tell you the truth to save your soul I decree this in Jesus name.
I declare that God is not trying to harm me but help me.
I decree that I am God creation in Jesus name.
Power is my legal right to fight spiritual warfare.
I will not allow a religious to tell me my sin is greater than there's I decree this in Jesus name.
I declare that Jesus is the reflection of God in my life.
God has revealed to my apostolic spirit that he is more than enough.
I decree that I'm not arrogant I just have Jesus on the inside of me.
I set my mind free from all religious mindset and I receive the mind of Christ.
I declare that God has always been real to me I have come too far to turn around in Jesus name.
I have given God a strong yes in Jesus name.

I decree that satan is my infernal enemy and is already defeated in Jesus name.
I decree that the enemy will not use my flesh to pull me away from God.

I Must Die To My Flesh

I decree that I will receive the blessings if I am in right standing with God.
I will not allow sin to block the revelation that God is trying to give me I decree this in Jesus name.
I declare that I have a responsibility to grace and I must stay in holiness and purification.
The sin that I do all week will keep me from receiving when I go to church.
I decree that the presence of God will demand my spirit and then I can receive a revelation from God.
I have matured in God and I don't need a confirmation on everything that he tells me I decree this in Jesus name.
I declare that God will come to my rescue but as I mature I have to wait this will increase my faith.
I decree that God has strengthened my belief system.
I declare that the hand on my spirit is my faith in God.
I believe in the authority given to me and I run after God's power I decree this in Jesus name.
I no longer will ask God to move the obstacles he has already given me the power to move all obstacles in my way.
I decree that I am one with Christ.
I will no longer allow my flesh to dictate to me.
I'm alert to every trick of deception from the enemy.
I cancel all demonic moves unseen and seen in my life in Jesus name.
I decree that I am already seated in heavenly places with Christ.
By being one with Christ I live like him and I look like him.
I will raise my level of faith in Jesus name.
I decree that while the church is following the crowd my church will follow the cloud in Jesus name.
I declare that Jesus wants to know who I am in him I decree I know Christ in the power of his resurrection.
I declare that I am Christ manifesting on earth in Jesus name.
The principalities of this world are not interested in moving me they want to kill the Christ in me.
I decree that daily life trials encourage me to be more like Christ and die to my flesh.

I decree that my spirit will stay in a place that Christ can reach me in Jesus name.
I declare that the world will not consume my mind in Jesus name.
I declare that I rejoice that my name is not just written in heaven it cannot be erased because I am one with Christ.

All Burdens Not Bad

I declare that not all burdens are negative burdens.
I thank God for allow certain situations in my life it moved me out of my comfortable area in Jesus name.
I decree as a leader in my church I have to pick up on the burdens of the church in Jesus name.
I refuse to allow anyone to turn the truth of God into a burden in Jesus name.
I declare that God raised me up to take on burdens to bring revival, restoration and close the gap in any breeches that the enemy tries to open.
God says he knows what my situation looks like and already sent an answer I decree this in Jesus name.
I decree that in this season the enemy is trying to tighten his grip on my life I will release the fire of God on every burden coming my way in Jesus name.
I declare that I will walk in victory and not let a season of darkness permeate me in Jesus name.
I decree that every saint must stand on their watch and not make excuses to what God called us to do.
Thank you God for prioritizing my time in Jesus name he needs me to guard and protect and not let the powers of darkness invade my heart and mind I decree this in Jesus name.
I decree that while I am on my watch I will not be afraid to tell people that sin is sin.
I will not let a spirit of religion put burdens upon me in Jesus name.
Father God open my eyes and expose all false burdens in Jesus name.
I decree that God called me to be more than a Sunday saint I need to catch up with the Holy Spirit in Jesus name.
I declare I must stand still and stop running from what God called me to do.
I will take the word of God that change my life back to those still stuck in the sin I was in.
I decree that my eyes are open to all destruction going on around me and I must stand in the gap and pray in Jesus name.

What God is Saying

God said I am pulling one layer of skin to put a new one on.
This is not a season to slack in your obedience.
Several transitions have taken place.
There is a apostolic grace is being released upon the saints.
Move with momentum, passion, commitment, clarity, and pursing anointing.
We must not fail this assignment.
There has been allot of sifting going on.
We have to be radical, ready, redeemed like never before.
Penetrate in places we have never been.
Penetrate to a new realm in our prophetic praise and have a servitude attitude, willing to be a risk taker.
Become a progressive and emotional praiser.
If people think that they have figured out our anointing they will not respect us.
Your praise is not pleasing to God go higher (stagnated).
God wants to sing back to us it only happens in prophetic praise/worship.
Flow with the river of God flowing in your church.
The devil is confused and can't find you in the spirit.
Penetrate in your prayers stop praying the same ole prayers.
Take a declarative anointing and speak in your prayers that you declare.
I'm not asking I'm releasing.
Pick up the burden of the Lord and pray for someone else.
If you can't pray like you used to God is trying to shift you.
Be very aggressive become a legislature.
Pray what God said speak his word.
If you don't change you are going to miss this season with God.
We are ambassadors for Christ.
God said the authority is in your voice to stop abortion, murder, drug selling etc.
You must have a war like mentality.
Tell the devil I'm a battle axe for the Lord.
Before it is said and done God is going to do all that he said he will do.
Of you don't penetrate to a new realm the realm that you are in will penetrate you (cause you to backslide).
If you allow people to abort you, you are the fool.
Don't let people get to you says God you are shifting.
Penetrate in your giving to get out of poverty.
Release prophetic decrees over your city, and nation to break demonic strongholds.
God is requiring unity among us.
You are your brother's keeper stop gossiping.

The move of God won't come unless there is unity.
Don't bring another spirit to this vision.
Speak to the spirit of laziness, stagnation, slothfulness and being lazy at what told you to do.
Speak to that robbery spirit that that's robbing you of your time, talent, and money.
In this region God is setting us up to be an apostolic resource center.
Prophetic leaders will come from all over (nations) to receive from us.
Technology will have a web cast for the nations.
We will cause revival in our nations/regions.
A house of healing for the wounded leader to put back order, counsel them, restore them.

What God Wants In This Season

I decree that God wants us to believe him for the supernatural in Jesus name.
I will believe God like never before there is no limit on what God can do.
I decree that God wants to release utterance to us so we can understand and know what we are talking about in Jesus name.
I know that I have been sent and God has a plan and purpose for my life.
I declare that I will catch the vision of my local house in Jesus name.
I decree that God is restoring the apostolic and prophetic in his church.
I will be in the place that God wants me to be so I can receive my healing, deliverance, and blessings in Jesus name.
I declare that Zion will be the people of God that will release his prophetic word in Jesus name.
I declare that God is pouring out his spirit on all flesh to prophesy his word.
I declare that the prophetic word over my child is coming to pass in this season.
I will daily release out of my mouth the word of God spoken over my offspring.
I declare that the devil is mad that he can't kill my child in Jesus name.
I decree that my child will make a liar out of every demonic word spoken over there life Jesus name.
I declare that I have broken all generational curses off my offspring in Jesus name.
I decree that God wants me to know that the tug in the spirit has been cancelled off my child in Jesus name.

I decree that a prophetic and aggressive anointing that will be released upon my seed a fresh anointing like never before.
I decree that God has honored all the days and nights that I have prayed for my children and this is going to cause me to shift higher in the spiritual realm in Jesus name.
I declare that I have opened the eyes to see the move of God on my children.
The devil might touch my child but he can't kill them in Jesus name.
I declare that my apostolic praise is the roar in the spiritual realm that my children need in Jesus name.
I will release a roar for everything that concerns me in Jesus name.
I declare that I will go into the lion's kingdom (devil) and roar there's something in my roar that won't let me stop praising in Jesus name.
I decree I will praise my child out of hell in Jesus name.
In Jesus name I declare this is what God wants me to know.

The Next Move Of God

I decree that the next move of God is going to save the drug dealer off the corner, stop the prostitute from being a whoremonger, take the taste of crack out of the mouths of the smokers, take the taste of liquor away from the alcoholic, stop the parent from abusing the innocent child, stop the father from molesting his daughter, stop the liar from lying, stop the gossiper from gossiping, put the millions into the kingdom minded church, stop the lust of money, stop the adultery, stop the fornicating, stop little girls from giving up their virginity in Jesus name.
I decree that the next move of God will teach young men and women their value in life in Jesus name.
I declare that the next move of God we will feel his presence like never before.
This is my hour to rise up and receive the harvest in this next move of God.
I decree that God has given us a double portion of discernment in Jesus name.
I decree that every time I speak I am writing something in the heavenlies and causing major change in Jesus name.
I declare that in this move of God I will not speak contrary to what God has spoken.
I decree that I will not allow anyone to write negativity into my life I will not receive the negative word they spoke against me in Jesus name.
I declare that my tongue is the pen of a ready writer in Jesus name.

In this move of God I decree that God wants me to write his word on my heart in Jesus name.
I declare that God wants me to command my morning every day and set the atmosphere in Jesus name.
In the next move of God he only wants me to speak what he say and not what I see in Jesus name.
I will not allow the devil to try to make me misinterpret the word of God I decree this in Jesus name.
I declare that God is releasing seed in this next move he wants to impregnate me in Jesus name.
I decree that I will protect my seed from the spirit of doubt in Jesus name.
I declare that I will abort all demonic babies sent over my life so those demonic words won't come to pass in Jesus name.
In this move of God he wants me to remind him of the word he spoke over me in Jesus name.

Promises For My Offspring

I decree that the enemy can't stop my children by destroying their future in Jesus name.
I have a promise from God.
I declare that if God by himself brought me out of darkness he can do the same for my offspring.
I decree that in spite of what the enemy is trying to do to my children God has already canceled his plans in Jesus name.
I curse every spirit of Lilith that is assigned to kill babies when the spirit sees that a champion has been born in the spirit realm in Jesus name.
I command the enemy to hear my voice and obey you will not kill babies before they are born in Jesus name.
The devil does not want a child to know their place in the kingdom I cancel that assignment now in Jesus name. Satan I decree that you cannot paralyze the mind of my child in Jesus name.
I decree that my child has identified themselves in the kingdom of God and know their assignment in Jesus name.
I decree that the devil don't care if they are male or female gender is not an issue to him his assignment is to kill, steal, and destroy the youth of this generation and I stand in the gap and take my place as a sniper in the spirit to stop him before he strikes in Jesus name.
I decree that my children will not grow up with a false identity; instead they will know that they are kings, and queens of the kingdom in Jesus name.

I decree that my children will not search outside of the will of God.
I decree that I can remember my past of not having a mother or father figure, no stability and never be allowed to be what God called me to be my children will never have to face this in Jesus name.
My Children will not believe the lies of the devil but the truth in God in Jesus name.
I decree that the devil will not stop my children from the high standard of God.
I declare that my child will not receive a tattoo of the skull and cross bone and come into demonic covenant with death in Jesus name.
I decree that I will tell my child to wait instead of giving him condoms in Jesus name.
I declare that my daughter/son are "Purity for Jesus".
I decree that kingdom people don't encourage their children to do things of the world in Jesus name.
I decree that I know what the heartache of the world is and don't want my child to go through with it.
I decree that I will watch the clothes with decals that my children will wear my child will not represent the kingdom of darkness in Jesus name.
I decree that I have to stay in God face about my children and not on Facebook in Jesus name.
I declare that the enemy will not shape and put a destiny on my offspring in Jesus name.
I decree that I show my child that I am living proof of what God can do in Jesus name.
I declare that I will practice what I believe in front of my kids in Jesus name.

God's Covenant

I decree that I will bring God's covenant back to the church who feel the covenant does not matter.
I declare that God wants us to walk in covenant agreement with him.
I decree that demonic javelins will be thrown at me when I walk in covenant with God. As long as I stay under the covering I am protected in Jesus name.
I understand that God operates out of covenant.
My covenant can cost me my life I must give all to God.
I decree that Jesus was the fulfillment of every covenant.

I declare that with my covenant I have a special agreement between me and God.
My covenant makes my spirit line up and become one with God.
I decree that if you don't walk in covenant you will have unnecessary problem in Jesus name
When you break you covenant here comes the devil.
I decree that I in this covenant forever.
I declare that my covenant with God will stop me from being a church hoper.
I decree that I must get grounded and rooted in my church.
I decree that God wants to root us in truth not in different doctrines.
I decree that my covenant carries responsibility in Jesus name.
I declare that an apostolic covenant produces stability.
When I'm in covenant with someone it's my job to help restore them and lift them up in Jesus name.
I will not make a covenant with God than break it I decree this in Jesus name.
I can't be in covenant with God and still shacking up, bar hoping, drink and smoking and go to church like nothing is happening.
I decree that I have to be in covenant with my church and I have to obey the voice of God.
I walk in humility and it makes me easy to receive correction in Jesus name.

I Have a Right To Be Free From My Past

I have a right to be free from my past in Jesus name.
I have a right to redemption in Jesus name.
I have a right to forget my wrongs of the past.
I have a right to forget I was a crack head, drug dealer, whoremonger, adulteress, a fornicator, a liar, a thief, a gang banger, a gossiper, a evil person, a witch/warlock, a prostitute, a jealous person, a solider for the devil in Jesus name.
I have a legal right to stay free in Jesus name.
I have a right to go back and rescue my friends who are still in the same sin I was in.
I have a right not to live in shame, guilt, condemnation, rejection, and confusion.
I have a right to hold my head up high I have been forgiven in Jesus name.
I have a right to receive the blessing of God.

I have a right to pray for my enemies.
I have a right to serve God because of my past.
I have a right to be free in my spirit in Jesus name.
I have a right to know that God took everything in me and made me who I am.
I have a right to worship God in spirit and truth.
I have a right to be a blessing to the kingdom of God.
I decree and declare this in Jesus name.

Dark Places of Rebellion

I decree that God does not play with sin so why should I.
I decree that I cannot purposely sin and be in fellowship with God.
God will let me be in a dark place and let me live so that I will obey him the next time around.
Father God please expose the sin in my life that I may do unknowingly in Jesus name.
My covenant will allow me to watch who and what is around me in Jesus name.
I decree that God will remove everyone in my life who will keep me in a dark place.
I declare that I will not hang with rebellious people in Jesus name.
I decree that dark things happen due to disobedience in Jesus name.
This is not a season for me to flip flop in Jesus name.
I declare that I will not let God down by being rebellious in Jesus name.
God is doing a fresh thing in my life and will bring new people into my life I decree this in Jesus name.
Every counterfeit person is exposed in my life every person on my outer court God will remove out of my path in Jesus name.
I decree that I am a gifted person with character in Jesus name.
I declare that I am not a person of character with compromise I do not act like the world when I'm alone in Jesus name.
My character has helped me produce and receive what God has for me.
I declare that my anointing will get me through the door and keep me in Jesus name.
Father God down load me with the character of Jesus.
I renounce all spirits of rebellion and witchcraft from my life in Jesus name.
I decree that I will watch what I hear and see that my invite the spirit of rebellion back to me in Jesus name.
I will not speak word curse over myself in Jesus name.

I decree that I know the area of my life that I need to keep under the blood in Jesus name.
Thank you for saving me from all dark places in Jesus name.

My Covenant Will Allow Me To

My covenant will allow me to speak life into a dark place.
I decree and declare that I have received the baptism of the Holy Spirit.
My covenant gives me the legal license to use the power of the baptism of the Holy Spirit.
I declare that I have the right to the power and authority that God has given me in Jesus name.
My covenant gives me power over kingdoms of darkness, government, arts and entertainment, my family, the media, the air waves that promote violence and death, and my nation.
I declare that I will use my anointing to pull down, destroy, build, and plant for the kingdom of God.
I will use my covenant to root out deeply seeded things in my nation and region; the traditional things that keep God's people in bondage and make his word have no effect in Jesus name.
I declare that I will up root the powers of darkness and stop the growth in my family, job, schools, universities, my region, religious spirits, and nation in Jesus name.
I decree that with my anointing I will uproot every negative word directed at myself, my family, my offspring, my church, my leader, the president of the United States.
I declare that with my covenant I will declare something different than what was spoken in Jesus name.
I decree that my covenant will allow me to pull down things that have been built on the wrong or demonic foundation, principalities, curses, perversion, territorial spirits, and demonic strongholds in Jesus name.
My covenant will allow a release from the heavenlies in Jesus name.
I declare that my covenant will allow me to defeat my enemy and come forth victorious in Jesus name.
I declare that my covenant breaks all satanic kingdoms, occult leaders, witches, warlocks, physic, necromancers, and seers in the demonic realm.
I decree that my covenant will allow me to build Gods kingdom, his ways, his language, and Gods culture here on earth in Jesus name.
My covenant will not build God's kingdom over mess in Jesus name.

I decree that I have my shovel in the realm of the spirit to uproot all demonic spirits in Jesus name.
My covenant will allow me to plant things spiritually that will never die.
I declare that God is into spiritual reformation in Jesus name.
I declare that my covenant will help me move strongly in the prophetic in Jesus name.
Father God I ask that you redig the wells, refresh your people and bring reformation in Jesus name.
I decree that God has given me grace to have territorial commitment to my church, city, and region and his grace helps me sustain in Jesus name.

Walking Blindly

I decree that if I don't hearken to the voice of the Holy Spirit I will be in spiritual blindness.
Thank you God for opening my eyes to spiritual truth in Jesus name.
I declare that now that my eyes are open to the truth I will be held accountable in Jesus name.
God will always give me his directions and will speak clearly to me I decree this in Jesus name.
Now that I see clearly God is revealing great things to me and I am not stagnated in Jesus name.
I will speak from the apostolic about the things of God that I see in Jesus name.
I decree that I will not do the will of God with anger but I will do his will with love.

A Breakthrough Believer

I decree that I will carry a spirit of faith, a spirit of wisdom, a spirit of revelation/knowledge, a spirit of understanding, a spirit of counsel in Jesus name.
I declare that as a breakthrough believer I can walk through all the hell in my life in Jesus name.
I will only give Godly counsel and I will only receive Godly counsel in Jesus name.
I declare that my life depends on Godly counsel.
I will not allow the opinions of others mess my walk up in Jesus name.

I trust God he knows the thoughts and plans that he has for my life.
I release a spirit of might upon myself that will enable me to do more in the natural in Jesus name.
I decree that God is going to use my life experiences to bring great breakthrough to me.
The attacks on my body God is going to use that to heal others in Jesus name.
When I leave my house I carry the spirit of breakthrough with me.
I declare that I am not just a church goer I'm a breakthrough believer in Jesus name.
I will receive the word of God and I will take it back to the streets with passion and spread God's word I decree this in Jesus name.
I declare that I will stand my ground and show the devil that I am not giving up.
As a breakthrough believer I will go outside of my territory and rescue souls for the kingdom in Jesus name.
The prophetic announcement was already made about me in the spiritual realm I decree this in Jesus name.
God has given me significant and sudden change and development in Jesus name.
I decree that I am what God says I am in Jesus name.
I want the fullness of God for my life in Jesus name.
I decree that I make announcements to myself I know how to encourage myself in Jesus name.
I declare that I will not live out of my feelings and flesh I will live by faith.
I decree that I will not give into the devil I work to be done in the nations.
I made a vow to God that I will carry his spirit to the nations in Jesus name.
I decree that I may have to toil for a moment and it may get tiresome but I will not give up on God in Jesus name.
I decree that God has given me a pioneering spirit to lay the foundation in Jesus name.
I declare that God is dealing with everything in me that is not of him that may hinder my walk as a breakthrough believer in Jesus name.
I decree that God has given me breakthrough so I can be effective in helping others.
If God said it, it shall come to pass I will not stop praying God hears my humble cry in Jesus name.
I decree that I will pull my dreams off the shelf and start believing again in Jesus name.
I may not have the money but I have the breakthrough in Jesus name.
In the spiritual realm I put up a sign telling the devil "Do not disturb".

I declare that I have shut the doors to poverty, lying, stealing, and laziness in Jesus name.
I decree that there are no doors like the one God opens up.

Move In A Strong Apostolic Relationship

I decree that God is delighted when we allow him to remove deeply seeded sin from our life in Jesus name.
I will not come into covenant with people who carry a foolish spirit in Jesus name.
I decree that I will come into covenant with people who are going the same direction as I am.
I'm like an eagle I am called to soar in the midst of storms and battles and never come down in Jesus name.
I declare that I will glide and shift with God in the spirit.
I will not be like a turkey and be full of excuses in Jesus name.
I decree that God has given me the eyes of an eagle to look through the storms that my natural eye can't see in Jesus name.
I decree that I will not hang with people who pull at me and never have a deposit and never encourage me in Jesus name.
I decree there is a protective measure between people who share a covenant.
I will bring help, protection, covering and speak into the lives of my friends in Jesus name.
I draw from people that I am in covenant with in Jesus name.
I decree if you come into my presence foolish you will leave with wisdom.
I declare there is nothing worth me losing my destiny and purpose in God.
I live to please God and not man I will live a holy life I declare this in Jesus name.
Because I live holy people in my presence will want to live holy.
I decree that I will not hang with people who speak condemnation about my past in Jesus name.
I will allow the Holy Spirit to split open my life to get to the root of my problems I declare this in Jesus name.
I will be on the lookout for seducing people who try to speak into my life, they have to qualify to speak over me and lay hands on me I decree this in Jesus name.
People who speak contrary to the word of God cannot speak into my life in Jesus name.

I decree that church people will try to mess up your anointing and tell you that you have not had a breakthrough; I silence the voice of the accuser in the name of Jesus.
I curse every agent of satan and stop there assignment against my life in Jesus name.
I declare that God did not birth me to be counterfeit in Jesus name.
I decree that I will not be boxed into religion and legalism in Jesus name.
In this season I will not reason with my fleshly desires in Jesus name.

Obedience in All

When people come into my presence they can see and hear the presence of God in me.
I decree that the enemy is always trying to hit me from every side that is why I stayed built up by prayer.
I declare that integrity and character is the measuring rod.
I ask myself am I kingdom minded.
I declare that I will connect my purpose to the voice of God.
I will release the word with the sound of God that is what makes the enemy mad my voice has influence in Jesus name.
I ask myself daily how committed am I to the assignment God has for me.
I declare that if someone is not in alignment with me they are not connected to me.
I decree that I will not be connected to the demonic things of this world in Jesus name.
The more that I am obedient the more God can trust me in Jesus name.
I thank God from pulling me out of the sin that I was in and using me to win souls because of my obedience I decree this in Jesus name.
I declare that I will never lose my fire for God.
The devil comes to challenge my faith and beliefs and the word of God that's inside of me I remind the devil that the word of God is infallible he can't steal what I believe I declare this in Jesus name.
I declare that God has appointed me and no one can stop that.
I'm committed to the assignment and God will add on I'm in alignment and connected to what is mine I decree this in Jesus name.
What's in God's hands man cannot pluck out and God hold me in the palm of his hand I declare this in Jesus name.
I declare that God keeps me from falling.

Breaking The Spirit of Limitations

I decree that we are called to release the fire of God in Jesus name.
I declare that God delivered me from my mess and is using me greatly for his kingdom.
I decree that as a breakthrough believer I need some obstacles in my way.
There is more in me than I think and it comes to surface when I go through the trials of life in Jesus name.
I declare that God has broken the limitations off of the church there is no more excuses in Jesus name.
I declare that I am breaking the limitations off of myself and I carry the spirit of a breakthrough believer in Jesus name.
I will not allow the spirit of persecution to squeeze out the church in Jesus name.
I curse the spirit of slander from trying to stop the move of God in Jesus name.
I declare that I have denied myself to follow Christ.
I decree there is only one name under the heavens and that name is "JESUS".
I cancel the assignment of the spirit of delusion that will want me to always think something is wrong I am anchored in what I believe I declare this in Jesus name.
I understand the depth of the darkness that God delivered me from in Jesus name I will not go back to sin I will go back to win the lost I decree this in Jesus name.
I declare that the persecution that came up against me God used it to bring spiritual breakthrough in Jesus name.
I remind the devil that it is not an option for me to backslide to be part of his kingdom in Jesus name.
God revealed to me that people want me to stay in their walls of limitation, so I would have to need them, run my life, and persecute me for the good that I am doing in Jesus name.
I decree that I have learned to shift with God and not man.
I decree that my focus is where I'm going and not where I have been I will not on to my mistakes and problems that I had in Jesus name.
I decree that breakthrough limitations are for advancement in Jesus name.
I'm going through right now not because God is mad at me there is a breakthrough in the making.
God has birthed oil in my life to give me a heavy anointing a strong conviction for when I do wrong I declare this in Jesus name.
I decree that what I am going through in 2012 is for my move in 2013.

I decree that the enemy can't kill me until he gets an appointment from God the death angel may come but he can't take my life in Jesus name.
Kingdom believers don't just die we have to complete the assignment that God has given to us I decree this in Jesus name.
God has given me a spirit of tenacity in Jesus name.
I'm chosen for this season and father God I ask that you only allow people in my pathway who have something to do with my assignment for you in Jesus name.

Mobilizing My Child For the Apostolic

I declare that when the joy of the Lord is my strength I will never run low.
The Holy Spirit is the best teacher that I have ever had I decree this in Jesus name.
I decree that I will measure everything that comes from God his word is the measuring rod.
I declare that as long as I stay lined up with God he will not only save me but my family also.
God will send me a prophetic word to me about my child so I will not worry God will bring my child to a place where they will openly praise him in Jesus name.
I decree that I will not leave my offspring behind they are going to be in the middle of the battle.
I decree that God is bringing every word I have prayed to past in Jesus name.
My children are coming out of circumstances and situations that only God will be able to pull them out of.
I declare that God will not allow the enemy to kill my offspring.
I decree that every snare and trap set for my child God is going to use it to deliver and mobilize my child in Jesus name.
God is mobilizing all of our children to send them back out into the darkness to be the light and flavor that the lost will need I decree this in Jesus name.
The Holy Spirit is busy trying to get my child's attention he heard my prayers and cries.
I decree that I will leave my child in the running place I can't be the fourth head in the God head.
I will not allow my child to give me a guilt trip in Jesus name.
God wants me to sit back and watch overnight how he will bring my child to a position to be a praiser.

I declare that God will allow the things of the world to hit them so they will call on him.
I cannot change what God has said I will line up to what God is saying I decree this in Jesus name.
I will daily remind my child what God has said about them in Jesus name.
I decree that I will not get nervous when the devil tries to kill my child he just wants me to believe that he has more power than God the devil is a liar.
The death angel cannot take your child make decrees and declarations over your child in Jesus name.
I declare that I live under the covenant and promises of God.
As long as I live what I preach in front of my child they will want to serve God I decree this in Jesus name.
I decree that I will not let my mind wonder when danger is near my child I will remember the word and my authority over the works of darkness.
I decree that I will not believe the words of the devil what God has proclaimed the devil can't stop it.
When people ask about my child I will say they are blessed and highly favored in Jesus name.
I decree that if God has to use my child behind bars they will preach the word in Jesus name.
I decree that I will keep my mind, will and emotions together in Jesus name.
God has built my spirit up so when troubles comes I can say peace be still in Jesus name.
I'm prepared to fight this war for my child in Jesus name.
I will draw near and not away from God in Jesus name.
I have what it takes to get the job done.
I decree that me and my child will go into the devils kingdom and wreak havoc in Jesus name.
I will make a prophetic act in the natural what was spoken in the spiritual.
I have been called out of darkness and I don't live in the dark anymore I decree this in Jesus name.
I declare that I am paving the path for my children's children in Jesus name.
I declare that my child will go into the world and touch places that I have not in Jesus name.
Me and my child have come from bondage to liberty I decree this in Jesus name.
I declare that God has mobilized my child for the warfare of this season in Jesus name.

What God Excepts From Me

I decree that the more God gives me the more he requires of me.
I have to be faithful with the least that God has given me before I can receive more in Jesus name.
I decree that I have to be faithful with the anointing that I have before God will give me a new one.
My faithfulness is my attributes, my righteousness, and concentration in Jesus name.
I decree that I will not allow the devil to run the altar in my mind.
I decree that Jesus took every excuse to the cross so that I would not have any.
I break every spirit of procrastination from me in the name of Jesus.
I will not focus on how I feel or what's around me my focus will be on how I can please God today.
I declare that this is my season for expansion and promotion in Jesus name.
I decree that if I am not faithful over the assignment in my local area, I will not be able to break through the principalities in Jesus name.
God wants me to pioneer into a greater breakthrough in Jesus name.
I declare that God wants me to go into places that I have never been in Jesus name.
I will keep my covenant with God so that I will not be distracted not to complete the assignment God has for me I decree this in Jesus name.
I declare that God expects me to work miracles and show the power of God to draw in the unbelievers in Jesus name.
I know the present God and the movement of God for this season God is raising me up quickly I decree this in Jesus name.
I decree that I will need the pioneering ability for a greater breakthrough in Jesus name.
I declare that God wants me to set things in motion, advance, gain grounds, take the lead, establish that what has never been established in the kingdom of God, and usher in his presence like never before.
I declare that God wants me to go into the tight places and bring breakthrough, God wants me to go in areas where the gospel has never been preached. God wants me to convert the Muslims to Christianity. God wants me to go into the prisons and stop our children from being under the doctrines of devils in Jesus name.
I declare that God is not limiting the church to one realm God is bringing the church to a new season in him.
I declare that God wants me to jump into the deep end in Jesus name.
I'm willing to let God be in control of my life in Jesus name.

I decree that God wants me to pull down the idols in the church in Jesus name.
I will not cry about the walls in my way I will stir up my pioneering spirit in Jesus name.
God has released a spirit of mite to go through in Jesus name.
I decree that I won't be afraid of the warfare that I am going through God is releasing a fearless anointing upon me in Jesus name.
I decree that holiness sets standard in my life in Jesus name.

Atmosphere For Encouraging Myself

I declare that I'm not in the earth realm just for nothing God has a plan and a purpose for me in Jesus name.
This is my season for divine appointment in Jesus name.
Just like David did I will learn to encourage myself in Jesus name.
I declare that I have received supernatural strength from God in Jesus name.
I will create an atmosphere of encouragement for myself and others in Jesus name.
Father God I ask that you strengthen me where I'm weak at in Jesus name.
I renounce every spirit of low self-esteem, rejection, self-hatred, and not loving myself in Jesus name I declare that I am loved, I am important, I am wanted, and that I am needed in Jesus name.
I decree that I will let my leaders know when I need encouragement in Jesus name.
I will fine tune my spirit with God spirit so I will know when he is present in Jesus name.
I decree that God will give me a word that can encourage me for a lifetime in Jesus name.
If I don't admit I need help how can I get to God.
I decree that what I am going through now is for the generation that is being built up for kingdom work in Jesus name.
I decree that I will spend time with what help deliver me in Jesus name.
God I ask that you remove whatever is between me and my transition in Jesus name.
I curse every spirit of doubt and fear that will keep me from encouraging myself in Jesus name.
I declare that everything that I am going through, God is going to see me through in Jesus name.
The weapon might form but it will not prosper in Jesus name.

I decree that God is not going to move the things that discourage me but he has given me the grace to sustain in Jesus name.
I command every church to deal with the demonic mindsets and bind and loose and bring deliverance in Jesus name.
The spirit of the Lord is in church waiting and looking for me in Jesus name.
I declare that my gift is not greater than the gift giver in Jesus name.
I will not become rebellious and sin against God.
I decree that God has already encouraged me in my distress in Jesus name.
I will not keep company with people who leave the church and carry a spirit of discouragement in Jesus name.
I cancel the assignment of anything that tries to drag me out of my place and purpose in Jesus name.
My testimony needs to be told to help encourage others who are going through.
I decree that I will never shut down what God called me to be I won't change my M.O. and compromise with sin.
I declare that as an apostle, elder, and a minister I can war in the spiritual realm, fight demonic battles, and conquer the kingdom of darkness in Jesus name.
I decree that ignorance is the biggest demon in churches; I bind every spirit of ignorance and remove all spiritual blindness, and deaf ears to the spirit of God. I lose the spirit of love, a sound mind, power, and the mind of Christ in Jesus name.
I speak to everybody that was called to be an apostle and I activate the apostle in you in Jesus name.
I declare that I will not listen to whispering demonic spirits in Jesus name.

Testing The Word Over Your Life

I decree that I will daily let the word spoken over me get into my spirit in Jesus name.
I will keep a notebook of all the prophecies spoken over me and I will check it off when it comes to past.
I decree that the devil will not stop the seed that has impregnated me he can't steal the word from my spirit in Jesus name.
I declare that God gives me his word to keep me encouraged so I don't get stuck.
I decree that just because the enemy has a legal right to go after the word God spoke over me I have the legal right to fight him back with the word of God.

I declare that my soul has to receive the word from God his word will speak me into my presence in Jesus name.
I will not allow the spirit of doubt to ask me how is God's word going to work in your life.
I decree that when God spoke his word in his eyesight it was already done all I have to do is bring my mind, will, and emotions together with the word from God.
I decree that I will daily remind my soul it is going to be what God said it would be in Jesus name.
In this season God is processing my soul for his word.
I will allow the Holy Spirit to work out his word in my life if I don't align myself than God will choose someone else in Jesus name.
I declare that there is a testing of the word over my life there is a responsibility that I have to fulfill
I decree that God is mantling me for a coat of many colors in Jesus name.
I will allow God to give me a spirit to interpret the dreams he has given me to show me of things to come.
I declare that the favor on my life is going to cause adversity from the people around me in Jesus name.
I declare that my garment has to be bloody (carried through the blood) in Jesus name.

Can God Use My Womb

I declare that the enemy will fight the name f Jesus when we call upon him in Jesus name.
This is a season where we will need boldness to fight religious demons I decree this in Jesus name.
I decree that I am not a baby saint I serve a big God and I'm allowing God to fully develop me.
I declare that in this season God is silencing people who put their mouth on me in Jesus name.
Father God I ask that you put a watch on my mouth so I don't speak against what God has said over me.
I decree that God wants to show me what he is doing and birthing out of me in Jesus name.
I declare that Mary carried the living word "Jesus" so why do we say women can't preach in Jesus name.
I decree that God gave me the womb of my mind so he can release his thoughts into me.

I decree that whatever seed I allow to grow is what seed I will speak from in Jesus name.
I decree that God gave me the womb of my heart I will not give my heart to everyone my heart is the intimate place where I meet God my heart has to stay clear in Jesus name.
I decree that I will watch what goes into my spirit through my eyes and ears in Jesus name.
I decree that I will learn to speak against the words that were spoken against me so I can enhance God's kingdom.
I decree that God made the church to be a womb I will speak abortion to every negative word spoken against the church in Jesus name.
I decree that my womb has to be right to be received.
I decree that there is no seed that can stop what God is doing in Jesus name.
I declare that you have to submit to the apostolic covering of your house (church) in Jesus name.
There is nothing in you that can make the apostolic negative in Jesus name.
I declare that I will be a front runner impregnating minds before the devil does in Jesus name.
I refuse to allow my church to grow with people who are pregnant with demonic babies.
I decree that my life has to be favorable in front of the Lord so that God can use me in Jesus name.
I will allow the seed of God to take root in my life in Jesus name.
I decree that I will not read the word of God and not do what it says.
God will drop seed, dreams, and visions into my womb I declare this in Jesus name.
I decree that God will use my womb to bring forth seed in Jesus name.
When I understand what I'm giving birth to that is in my womb my life will have more pleasure in Jesus name.
I decree that the war that is inside of me is the seed of God that the seed of the enemy is trying to attack.
I decree that my womb carries deliverance for the nations.

What Makes You Apostolic

I decree that I will not build a mindset to make me believe that I am not apostolic.
I will not allow a religious spirit put doubt in my mind about being apostolic and what I am called to do in Jesus name.

I declare that I am commissioned to apostolic.
I decree that I have to go through discipleship so I can function in the fullest in Jesus name.
I am sent forth to delegate be a messenger, sent forth as a commissioner of Christ I have been given by the Holy Spirit with a particular anointing I decree this in Jesus name.
I decree that I am sent forth to establish God's dominion on earth I will conquer every demonic territory in Jesus name.
I have been called forth with a diplomatic anointing in Jesus name.
I decree that I have the power of persuasion in Jesus name.
I'm called to lead the lost into the new frontier of the kingdom of God in Jesus name.
I decree that I am going forth with the mindset to conquer in Jesus name.
I decree that I will not allow my personal life to interfere with God's work.
I decree that I am dead to my flesh and my persecution shows it in Jesus name.
To be caught up into the third heaven is the thorn in your side in Jesus name.
I decree that I need a Judas spirit around me to build more character in me.
I declare that my gift will take me there and my character will keep me there in Jesus name.
I walk in the patience of an apostolic person in Jesus name.
God has given me the grace to walk in a cheerful endurance I decree that in Jesus name.

The Announcement Has Been Made

I declare that I am the modern day John the Baptist sent to prepare the way.
I decree that God has to be well please with me in order to move in this season.
I live from the proceeding word of God.
I declare that there has been an announcement made about me in the heavenlies the enemy wants me to think that it will not come to past in Jesus name.
The power of the baptism confirms me in Jesus name.
I decree that all marine spirits (Leviathan) heard the announcement concerning me.
I declare that I know who I am in God and the devil cannot turn me away from my identity in Jesus name.

I decree that I need God in the midst of my trials and I will hold on to every word that God has spoken about me.
I have the faith to believe what God says I decree this in Jesus name.
I decree that the devil wants to fight the things that God says about me.
I will not live from the bread of this world I will live from the heavenlies in Jesus name.
I declare that I am not troubled, destroyed, or confused in Jesus name.
I declare that I am living from a realm where everything I need is provided for me.
The angels from heaven will assist me into getting the job done in Jesus name.
I praise God for the announcement that was made over me.

Walking Through My Open Door

I decree that worship reveals who sits on the throne of my heart.
I declare that I can't switch seasons and wear my old garments in Jesus name.
I decree that I will bring my mind to a new place of advancement in Jesus name.
In my new season I will use new and different war tactics in Jesus name.
I declare that if I can't discern seasons I will not be able to walk through the open doors God has for me.
I declare that I am in a season of more than enough and I will not speak from the season of not enough.
In Jesus name I will not let anyone keep me from my open doors.
I declare that I will not allow my anointing to get cold while I'm in my new season.
I will not miss my divine opportunity or moment with God I decree this in Jesus name.
I decree that I'm in the new seasons as other but I don't walk like them in Jesus name I am not a complainer.
I'm walking through the hallway of the adversary and no demon in hell can stop me in Jesus name.
I declare that the warfare that I go through is trying to show me what I keep missing this is not my season to go in circles in Jesus name.
I declare that I will stop letting my haters take me through the wrong doors in Jesus name.

I decree that in my new season I will not be looking back at what people think, say or feel about me I will bless and pray for those who just tolerate me in Jesus name.

I'm in the season where death is all around me but I stand in the doorway of love in Jesus name.

I declare that in this season God wants me to work for my new door so when I walk through no devil in hell or human devil in my pathway can take it away from me in Jesus name.

I refuse to let what someone says hinder me from walking through my open door.

I declare that I have to walk and pray from door to door I will not leave a door open for just in case things don't work out in Jesus name.

I declare that there is hell in the hallways between my open doors in Jesus name.

I decree that I am in the hallway of my blessings in Jesus name.

I decree that I'm not going backwards but I'm going through the doors God opens.

I declare that I already have the master keys the keys to the kingdom in Jesus name.

The key to my mind is worship in Jesus name.

I decree that the next doorway is where God is going to make my name great in Jesus name.

I declare that by the end of 2012 I'm walking through every door that God has for me in Jesus name.

CPSIA information can be obtained
at www.ICGtesting.com
Printed in the USA
FFOW02n0953241117
43735094-42606FF